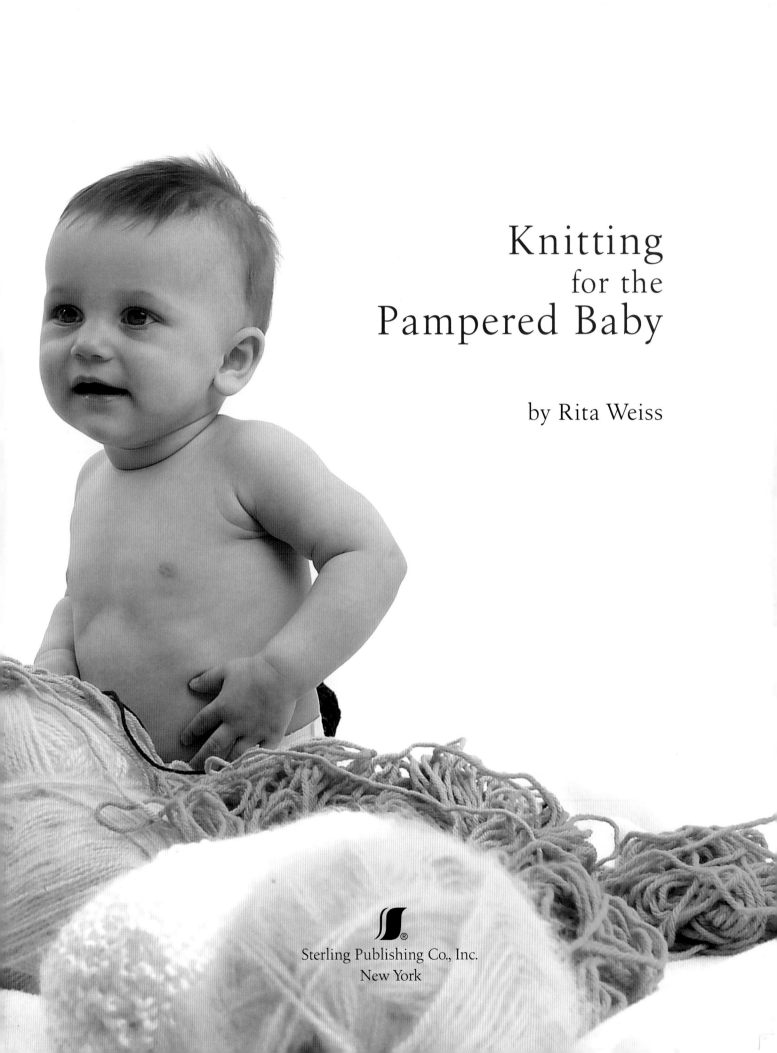

Knitting
for the
Pampered Baby

by Rita Weiss

Sterling Publishing Co., Inc.
New York

Library of Congress Cataloging-in-Publication Data Available

2   4   6   8   10   9   7   5   3   1

Published by Sterling Publishing Co., Inc.
387 Park Avenue South, New York, NY 10016
© 2005 by The Creative Partners, LLC™
Distributed in Canada by Sterling Publishing
c/o Canadian Manda Group, 165 Dufferin Street
Toronto, Ontario, Canada M6K 3H6
Distributed in Great Britain by Chrysalis Books Group PLC
The Chrysalis Building, Bramley Road, London W10 6SP, England
Distributed in Australia by Capricorn Link (Australia) Pty. Ltd.
P.O. Box 704, Windsor, NSW 2756, Australia

Printed in China

Sterling ISBN 1-4027-1375-4

Introduction

For a long time we thought that creating these little garments for the pampered babies in our lives was fun.

Then we met the babies, and we discovered the real meaning of fun.

They arrived, bundled to the hilt, on a cold winter's day, making their way across town to the large room we had picked for shooting. Our photographer was prepared, the lights were at ready, we had toys and goodies in waiting. We were not prepared, however, for the babies and the absolute joy and warmth they would bring into the room in what could have been a difficult situation.

Each child displayed a unique personality, and those personalities are very evident in the pictures in this book. There was the super serious little girl who refused to smile no matter how many funny faces were made off-camera. There was the wandering boy who was completely mesmerized by a group of toy trains we had brought along and another who became attached to a pair of toy horses. One little girl at first refused to pose, and then, upon discovering that she could be the center of attention, pushed the other children off the set so that she could be photographed in every garment. There was the daddy who convinced his daughter it would be fun by wearing the sample hat for an hour so that she would want to be photographed in it. And, there were the babies who needed no prodding when we plopped them down in a pile of yarn. That was fun!

We hope the photographs will give you an idea of how precious these garments are; how perfect they are—not for just any baby—but for that pampered baby, that special baby in your life.

Can't remember how to knit? Confused as to what those abbreviations and symbols mean? Spend a little time with our "Refresher Course" starting on page 120 and then knit one of the projects from this book. Once you present any one of these you've made to a child, you have created your own pampered baby.

Contents

STEPPING OUT IN STYLE
10

SUMMERTIME HOODIE
12

BABY FISHERMAN
14

**FOR A SPECIAL BABY
ON A SPECIAL DAY**
16

WHITE IS RIGHT
18

PRECIOUS PARKA
20

LITTLE FASHIONISTA
22

ALL DRESSED UP
24

REACH FOR THE STARS
26

TIME TO SUIT UP
28

SPECIAL FOR SNOW TIME
30

RAINBOW COAT
32

**CHRISTENING DRESS
& BONNET**
34

BABY KIMONO SWEATER
36

BERIBBONED AFGHAN
38

**LITTLE GUY'S
NORWEGIAN SWEATER**
40

THE LITTLE BLACK DRESS
42

**OLD-FASHIONED
BABY LAYETTE**
44

ANGEL TOP
46

CRAYON STRIPES
48

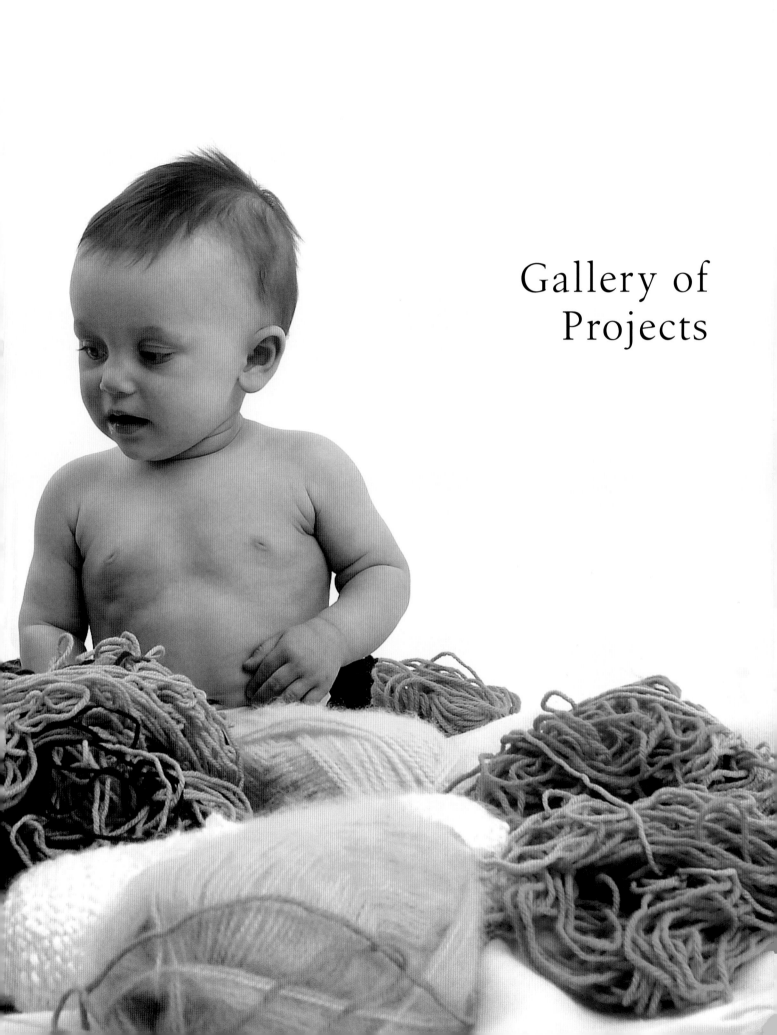

Gallery of
Projects

STEPPING OUT IN STYLE

Designed by Sandy Scoville

What little girl wouldn't enjoy wearing this colorful hat and coat set, featuring a beautiful smocked yoke? She'll be full of smiles all the way to the playground.

PATTERN APPEARS ON PAGE 52

SUMMERTIME HOODIE

Just the right weight and colors for summer, this boldly striped hooded sweater is perfect for that cool kid, either a boy or a girl.

PATTERN APPEARS ON PAGE 58

BABY FISHERMAN

The wonderful textures of classic aran knitting stitches are featured in this tiny version of a traditional sweater.

PATTERN APPEARS ON PAGE 60

FOR A SPECIAL BABY ON A SPECIAL DAY

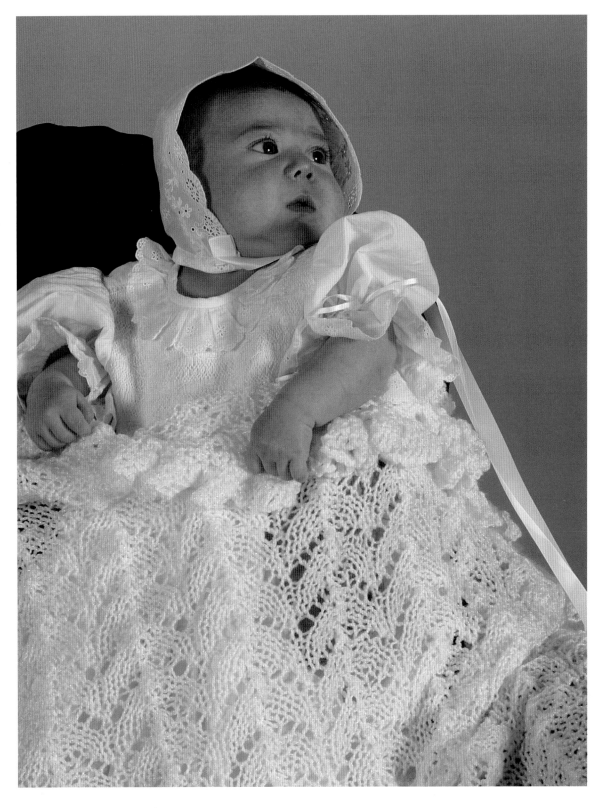

The perfect addition to a Christening ceremony, this lovely and lacey afghan with its crocheted ruffled border welcomes a new life into the world.

PATTERN APPEARS ON PAGE 64

WHITE IS RIGHT

Designed by Susie Adams Steele

She may be young, but she is still very fashion conscious. She's sure to feel all eyes on her when she dresses up in this charming sweater and skirt created in fashion's favorite white.

PATTERN APPEARS ON PAGE 66

PRECIOUS PARKA

*Neither sleet nor snow,
nor winter's chilly winds will
bother the child dressed in
this soft, furry parka.*

PATTERN APPEARS ON PAGE 70

LITTLE FASHIONISTA

Designed by Sandy Scoville

If you won't knit this trendy vest and hat, our little girl might just knit it for herself so that she can make a fashion statement.

PATTERN APPEARS ON PAGE 72

ALL DRESSED UP

Designed by Sandy Scoville

This darling yellow dress trimmed in lace will be the perfect outfit to wear anywhere that our little girl needs to star.

PATTERN APPEARS ON PAGE 76

REACH FOR THE STARS

Designed by Sandy Scoville

There are plenty of pockets in this charming pullover for tiny treasures, including any tiny objects little ones like to collect.

PATTERN APPEARS ON PAGE 80

TIME TO SUIT UP

Designed by Sandy Scoville

Isn't he cute in his matching shirt and pants!

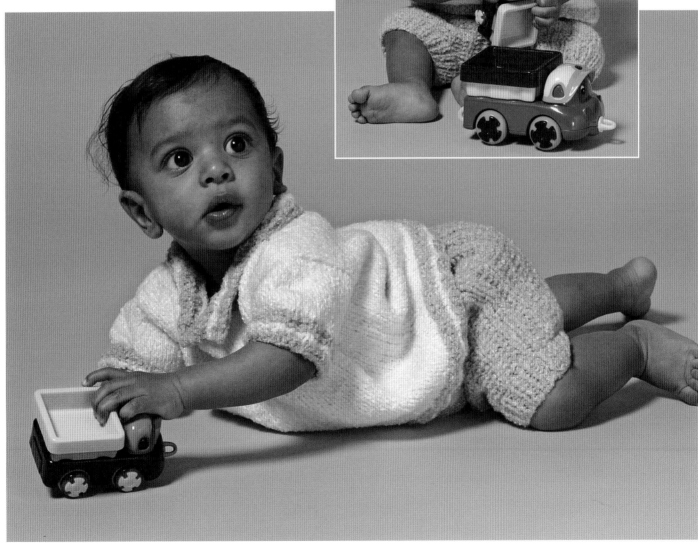

PATTERN APPEARS ON PAGE 82

SPECIAL FOR SNOW TIME

Let the winds blow! Tiny heads and hands are protected from the cold when they wear this muff and beret.

PATTERN APPEARS ON PAGE 86

RAINBOW COAT

Designed by Susie Adams Steel

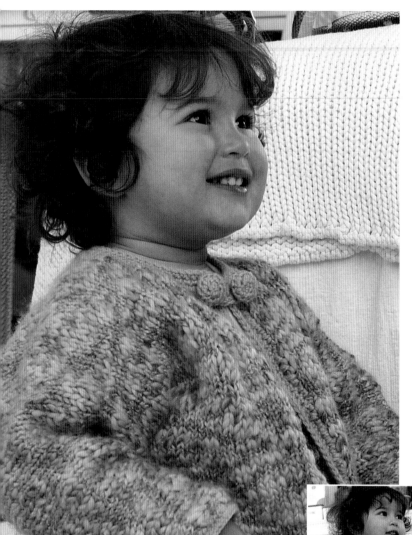

*Easy on, easy off, and easy to wear!
This comfy, cozy coat is perfect for
those cool Spring days.*

PATTERN APPEARS ON PAGE 88

CHRISTENING DRESS & BONNET

Designed by Jodi Lewanda

A true heirloom created in cashmere and silk, this Christening dress will become a family treasure.

PATTERN APPEARS ON PAGE 92

BABY KIMONO SWEATER
Designed by Susie Adams Steele

Bright colors are fun to wear for any little child.

PATTERN APPEARS ON PAGE 95

BERIBBONED AFGHAN

Soft and warm, this afghan is sure to be a favorite of any little one.

PATTERN APPEARS ON PAGE 98

LITTLE GUY'S NORWEGIAN SWEATER

Tradition can come in all sizes, even for small boys.

PATTERN APPEARS ON PAGE 100

THE LITTLE BLACK DRESS

Designed by Kim Britt

That little black dress belongs in every girl's wardrobe no matter what her age, and this one is especially soft and velvety.

PATTERN APPEARS ON PAGE 104

OLD-FASHIONED BABY LAYETTE

Every baby deserves a traditional layette made up of bonnet and booties along with a sweater and afghan. This one is really soft and cuddly,

PATTERN APPEARS ON PAGE 106

ANGEL TOP

A soft top for your little angel, this little dress can be worn alone or added to the old-fashioned baby layette.

PATTERN APPEARS ON PAGE 112

CRAYON STRIPES

All dressed up in a complete wardrobe of bright stripes.

PATTERN APPEARS ON PAGE 114

Patterns

STEPPING OUT IN STYLE

Designed by Sandy Scoville

Coat Sizes:	12 months	18 months	24 months
Body Chest Measurements:	20"	21"	22"
Finished Garment Chest Measurement:	22"	23"	24"

Note: *Instructions are written for size 12 months; changes for larger sizes are in parentheses.*

Bonnet Size:
One size fits 18"–19" circumference head

MATERIALS
Sport weight yarn,
    8 3/4 (10, 10) oz blue
    1 oz lime
Note: *Photographed model was made with Patons® Look at Me, Colors #6367 Bright Blue and #6362 Green Apple*
24" Size 5 (3.75 mm) circular knitting needle (or size required for gauge)
Size 18 tapestry needle
Six (six, seven) 3/8" buttons
Sewing needle and matching thread
One yd 3/8" wide lime green satin ribbon (for bonnet)

GAUGE
6 sts = 1" in stockinette st
    (knit one row, purl one row)

Coat Instructions
BACK
Starting at lower edge with blue, cast on 82 (86, 90) sts; do not join, work back and forth in rows.

Row 1 (right side)**:** Knit

Row 2: Purl.

Rows 3 through 6: Rep Rows 1 and 2.

Row 7 (eyelet turning row)**:** K1; * YO, K2 tog; rep from * to last st; K1.

Row 8: Purl.

Rows 9 through 20: Rep Rows 1 and 2.

Rows 21 and 22: Knit. At end of Row 22, cut blue.

For Size 12 Months Only:
Row 23: With lime, knit to last st; inc (knit in front and back of next st): 83 sts. Continue with Row 24.

For Size 18 Months Only:
Row 23: With lime, knit: 86 sts. Continue with Row 24.

For Size 24 Months Only:
Row 23: K2 tog; knit across: 89 sts. Continue with Row 24.

Row 24 (all sizes)**:** Purl.

Row 25: K1; * YO, sl 1 as to purl, K2, PSSO2; rep from * to last st; K1.

Row 26: Purl.

Rows 27 through 30: Rep Rows 25 and 26 twice. At end of Row 30, cut lime.

Rows 31 and 32: With blue, knit.

Row 33: Inc; knit to last st; inc: 85 (88, 91) sts.

Row 34 (all sizes)**:** Purl.

Continue in stock st until piece measures 11" (11", 12"), ending by working a wrong-side row.

UNDERARM SHAPING

Row 1 (right side)**:** Bind off 5 sts; K2; * P2, K1; rep from * to last 6 sts; K6: 80 (83, 86).

Row 2: Bind off 5 sts; P2; * K2, P1; rep from * to last st; P1: 75 (78, 81) sts.

BACK BODICE

Row 1 (right side)**:** K2; * P2, K1; rep from * to last st; K1.

Row 2: P2; * K2, P1; rep from * to last st; P1.

Rep Rows 1 and 2 until armhole measures 4" (4", 4½"), ending by working a wrong-side row.

Bind off.

LEFT FRONT

Starting at lower edge with blue, cast on 39 (41, 43) sts; do not join, work back and forth in rows.

Row 1 (right side)**:** Knit.

Row 2: Purl.

Rows 3 through 6: Rep Rows 1 and 2.

Row 7 (eyelet turning row)**:** * K2 tog; YO; rep from * to last st; K1.

Row 8: Purl.

Rows 9 through 20: Rep Rows 1 and 2.

Rows 21 and 22: Knit. Cut blue.

For Size 12 Months Only:
Row 23: With lime; K2 tog; K37: 38 sts. Continue with Row 24.

For Size 18 Months Only:
Row 23: With lime, knit: 41 sts. Continue with Row 24.

For Size 24 Months Only:
Row 23: Inc (knit in front and back of next st); knit across: 44 sts. Continue with Row 24.

Row 24 (all sizes)**:** Purl.

Row 25: K1; * YO, sl 1 as to purl, K2, PSSO2; rep from * to last st; K1.

Row 26: Purl.

Rows 27 through 30: Rep Rows 25 and 26 twice. At end of Row 30, cut lime.

continued on page 54

Row 2: Bind off first 10 sts; work in patt across: 23 (26, 29) sts.

Row 3: Work in patt to last 2 sts; K2 tog: 22 (25, 28) sts.

Row 4: P2 tog tbl; work in patt across: 21 (24, 27) sts.

Rows 5 through 10 (12, 14): Rep Rows 3 and 4. At end of Row 10 (12, 14): 15 (16, 17) sts.

Continue in patt without dec until left front measures same as back.

Bind off.

RIGHT FRONT

Work same as left front to underarm shaping.

RIGHT FRONT BODICE AND UNDERARM SHAPING

Row 1 (right side)**:** K2; * P2, K1; rep from * to last 6 sts; K6.

Row 2: Bind off 5 sts; P2; * K2, P1; rep from * to last st; P1: 33 (36, 39) sts.

Row 3: K2; * P2, K1; rep from * to last st; K1.

Row 4: P2; * K2, P1; rep from * to last st; P1.

Rows 5 through 22 (22, 26): Rep Rows 3 and 4.

RIGHT FRONT NECKLINE AND SHOULDER SHAPING

Row 1 (right side)**:** Bind off first 10 sts; work in patt across: 23 (26, 29) sts.

Row 2: Work in patt to last 2 sts; P2 tog tbl: 22 (25, 28) sts.

Row 3: K2 tog tbl; work in patt across: 21 (24, 27) sts.

Rows 4 through 9 (11, 13): Rep Rows 2 and 3. At end of Row 9 (11, 13): 15 (16, 17) sts.

STEPPING OUT IN STYLE
continued

Rows 31 and 32: With blue, knit.

Row 33: Knit.

Row 34: Purl.

Continue in stock st until piece measures same as back to underarm shaping.

LEFT FRONT BODICE AND UNDERARM SHAPING

Row 1 (right side)**:** Bind off 5 sts; K2; * P2, K1; rep from * to last st; K1: 33 (36, 39) sts.

Row 2: P2; * K2, P1; rep from * to last st; P1.

Row 3: K2; * P2, K1; rep from * to last st; K1.

Row 4: P2; * K2, P1; rep from * to last st; P1.

Rows 5 through 22 (22, 26): Rep Rows 3 and 4.

LEFT FRONT NECKLINE AND SHOULDER SHAPING

Row 1 (right side)**:** Work in patt across.

Continue in patt without dec until right front measures same as back.

Bind off.

SLEEVE (make 2)

With blue, cast on 40 (40, 42) sts; do not join, work back and forth in rows.

Row 1 (right side): Knit.

Row 2: Purl.

Rows 3 through 6: Rep Rows 1 and 2.

Row 7 (eyelet turning row): K1; * YO, K2 tog; rep from * to last st; K1.

Row 8: Purl.

Rows 9 and 10: Rep Rows 1 and 2.

Rows 11 and 12: Knit. At end of row 12, cut blue.

For Sizes 12 and 18 Months Only:
Row 13: With lime, knit to last st; inc (knit in front and back of next st): 41 (41) sts. Continue with Row 14.

For Size 24 Months Only:
Row 13: With lime, inc (knit in front and back of next st); K40; inc: 44 sts. Continue with Row 14.

Row 14 (all sizes): Purl.

Row 15: K1; * YO, sl 1 as to purl, K2, PSSO2; rep from * to last st; K1.

Row 16: Purl.

Rows 17 through 20: Rep Rows 15 and 16 twice. At end of Row 20, cut lime.

Rows 21 and 22: With blue, knit.

Row 23: Inc (knit in front and back of next st); knit to last st; inc: 43 (43, 46) sts.

Row 24: Purl.

Row 25: Knit.

Row 26: Purl.

Rows 27 through 54: Rep Rows 23 through 26 seven times more. At end of Row 54: 57 (57, 60) sts.

Row 55: Purl.

Continue in stock st until sleeve measures 10" (10", 10½").

Bind off.

SMOCKING

Smocking, which gives the honeycomb look, is worked with lime yarn in a tapestry needle, in vertical rows.

Smocking Back Yoke

Starting at lower right corner of back yoke, use contrasting thread or yarn and draw it through every fourth row, starting three rows above bottom edge

55

continued on page 56

STEPPING OUT IN STYLE

continued

of yoke, and working from right to left. This will indicate where smocking sts are to be worked as shown in the diagram.

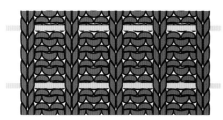

Step 1: Thread 18″ strand lime yarn into a tapestry needle. To begin smocking at lower right corner of back yoke, fasten yarn securely on wrong side and bring needle up to right of first knit st on 3rd row from yoke bottom edge; skip the next two purl sts to the left, and bring needle down to left of next knit stitch. Draw two knit sts tog and secure on wrong side.

Step 2: Bring needle up to right of first knit stitch in next marked row above, skip the two purl sts to the left, and bring needle down again to left of next knit stitch.

Continue in this manner vertically to neckline; finish off lime.

Step 3: Now go back to bottom edge of back yoke, skip the next two purl sts. Secure yarn on wrong side and bring needle up to right of next knit stitch to left, skip two purl sts, take needle down to left of next knit st, and draw together as before. Continue in this manner vertically, working on marked rows, to neckline.

Continue to work in this manner across entire back yoke.

Step 4: Return to right bottom of yoke. With lime yarn in needle, work in same manner vertically, now between previously marked rows and linking knit sts as shown in Photo.

Complete back yoke in this manner.

Smocking Front Yokes

Work as for back yoke, adjusting rows to work around neck shaping.

With blue, sew shoulder seams.

COLLAR

Row 1 (right side)**:** Hold coat with wrong side facing; beg at center left front edge, pick up and knit an even number of sts, having 2 sts for every 3 rows along front neckline, one st in each st across back, and 2 sts for every 3 rows to right center front edge.

Row 2: Purl.

Row 3: Knit.

Row 4: Purl.

Rows 5 through 12 (12, 14): Rep Rows 3 and 4.

Row 13 (15) (eyelet turning row)**:** K1; * YO, K2 tog; rep from * to last st; K1.

Row 14 (16): Purl.

Rows 15 through 24 (26): Rep Rows 3 and 4.

Bind off, leaving a 24″ end for sewing.

Fold Collar at eyelet row; with tapestry needle and long end, sew last row to wrong side of first row. Tack each front corner to front.

With blue, sew sleeves to body; sew underarm and side seams.

With blue, hem body and sleeves, turning lower edges to wrong side at eyelet row.

BUTTON PLACKET

Hold left front with right side facing and bodice at right.

Row 1 (right side)**:** With blue, pick up 2 sts for every 3 rows along center front edge; do not work into turned part of hem.

Row 2: Purl.

Row 3: Knit.

Rows 4 and 5: Rep Rows 2 and 3.

Row 6: Purl.

Row 7 (turning row)**:** Purl.

Rows 8 through 11: Rep Rows 2 and 3.

Bind off, leaving a 24″ end for sewing.

Turn placket at turning row; with tapestry needle and long end, sew to wrong side of Row 1.

BUTTONHOLE PLACKET

Hold right front with right side facing and bodice at left.

Row 1 (right side): Beginning at lower edge with blue, pick up 2 sts for every 3 rows along center front edge; you must have at least 70 (70, 79) sts.

Row 2: Purl.

Row 3: K12; bind off next 2 sts: buttonhole made; * K7, bind off next 2 sts: buttonhole made; rep from * 4 (4, 5) times more; knit rem sts.

Row 4: * Purl to buttonhole; cast on 2 sts; rep from * 5 (5, 6) times more; P12.

Row 5: Knit.

Row 6: Purl.

Row 7 (turning row): Purl.

Row 8: Purl.

Row 9: Knit.

Row 10: Purl until 59 (59, 68) sts rem on left needle, bind off next 2 sts: buttonhole made, * P7, bind off next 2 sts for buttonhole; rep from * 4 (4, 5) times more, P12.

Row 11: * Knit to next buttonhole, cast on 2 sts; rep from * 5 (5, 6) times more. Knit rem sts.

Rows 10 and 11: Rep Rows 3 and 4.

Row 12: Purl.

Bind off, leaving a 24″ end for sewing.

Turn placket at turning row; with tapestry needle and end, sew to wrong side of Row 1.

With sewing needle and matching thread, sew buttons opposite buttonholes. Sew tog edges of front and back layers around each buttonhole.

Bonnet Instructions

Beginning at front edge with blue, cast on 68 sts; do not join, work back and forth in rows.

Row 1 (right side): Knit.

Row 2: Purl.

Rows 3 through 6: Rep Rows 1 and 2.

Row 7 (eyelet turning row): K1; * YO, K2 tog; rep from * to last st; K1.

Row 8: Purl.

Rows 9 and 10: Rep Rows 1 and 2.

Rows 11 and 12: Knit. At end of row 12, cut blue.

Row 13: With lime, knit.

Row 14: Purl.

Row 15: K1; * YO, sl 1 as to purl, K2, PSSO2; rep from * to last st; K1.

Row 16: Purl.

Rows 17 through 20: Rep Rows 15 and 16 twice. At end of Row 20, cut lime.

Rows 21 through 23: With blue, knit.

Row 24: Purl.

Rows 25 through 46: Rep Rows 23 and 24.

Row 47: Bind off first 5 sts; knit across: 63 sts.

Row 48: Bind off first 5 sts; purl across: 58 sts.

Rows 49 and 50: Rep Rows 47 and 48. At end of Row 50: 48 sts.

Row 51: Bind off 10 sts; knit across: 38 sts

Row 52: Bind off 10 sts; purl across: 28 sts

Row 53: Knit.

Row 54: Purl.

Rep Rows 53 and 54 until piece measures 10″ from cast-on edge. Bind off.

FINISHING

Step 1: Fold front edge to wrong side at eyelet row; sew in place.

Step 2: With wrong sides held together, sew sides of center piece to bind-off rows, forming bonnet.

NECK RIBBING

Row 1 (right side): Hold bonnet with right side facing and lower edge at top; pick up and knit, having an even number of sts, 2 sts for every 3 rows along side edges, and one st in each bound-off st along center back.

Row 2: * P1, K1; rep from * across.

Rows 3 through 6: Rep Row 2.

Bind off in ribbing.

Cut ribbon into 2 equal lengths; make bow in at one end of each length. With sewing needle, tack one bow to each side of bonnet on ribbing at front edge.

SUMMERTIME HOODIE

Sizes:	24 months	36 months
Finished Garment Chest Measurement:	28″	30″

Note: *Instructions are written for size 24 months; changes for size 36 months are in parentheses.*

MATERIALS

Sport-weight yarn,

2 oz cream

1 ½ oz orange

1 ½ oz fuschia

1 ½ oz lilac

1 ½ oz yellow

1 ½ oz green

Note: *Photographed model was made with Lion Brand Microspun, Colors #910 French Vanilla; #186 Mango (orange); #146 Fuschia; #144 Lilac; #138 Buttercup, and #194 Lime.*

14″ Size 4 (3.5 mm) straight knitting needles (or size required for gauge)

14″ Size 5 (3.75 mm) 10″ straight knitting needles

GAUGE

5 sts and 8 rows = 1″ with larger needles in stockinette st (knit one row, purl one row)

Instructions

BACK

With smaller needles and cream cast on 70 (74) sts. Work K1, P1 ribbing for six rows.

Switch to larger needles and work in stock st in the following color sequence:

6 rows orange

2 rows cream

6 rows fuschia

2 rows cream

6 rows lilac

2 rows cream

6 rows yellow

2 rows cream

6 rows light green

2 rows cream

Repeat stripe pattern until back measures about 14″(15)″ from cast on edge. Bind off.

FRONT

Work same as back until the front measures 2 inches less than the back, ending by working a wrong-side row.

Dividing Row: Keeping stripe patt as established, K23 (24) for left shoulder; bind off 24 (26) for center front; join new yarn and work to the end of the row for right shoulder.

From now on, work in stock st in color pattern, using separate yarn for each shoulder, as follows:

Bind off one st at each neck edge every other row 3 times, then every 4th row twice: 18 (19) sts on each side. Work in pattern until front measures same as the back. Bind off.

SLEEVES (make 2)

With smaller size needles and cream cast on 38 (40) sts. Work K1, P1, ribbing for six rows. Switch to larger needles and orange.

Row 1: Inc in first st (to inc, knit in front and back of same st); knit to last st, inc in last st: 40 (42) sts.

Row 2: Purl.

Following color pattern, work in stock st, increasing one st at each end of needle every 5 rows 9 (10) times more: 58 (62) sts. Work even in pattern until piece measures 9" (10") from cast-on edge. Bind off.

HOOD

With larger needles and orange, cast on 38 (40) sts. Work in stock st in color patt until hood measures about 18" from cast on edge. Bind off.

FINISHING

Sew shoulder seams. Sew sleeves into armholes. Sew sleeve and side seams.

Fold hood in half and sew tog along long side.

Pin hood to neckline, starting and ending at center front, to fit neck edge; sew easing in place.

BABY FISHERMAN

Size:	3 years
Finished Garment Chest Measurement:	22"

MATERIALS

Sport weight wool-blend yarn,
  12 oz Off-white

Note: Photographed model was made with Lion Brand Wool-Ease® Sportweight, Color #099 Fisherman

14" Size 5 (3.75 mm) straight knitting
  needles (or size required for gauge)
14" Size 4 (3.5 mm) straight knitting
  needles
24" Size 4 (3.5 mm) circular knitting
  needles
Stitch markers
Cable needle
Four stitch holders
Tapestry needle

GAUGE

5 sts = 1" with larger needle in
  stockinette st (knit one row,
  purl one row)

PATTERN STITCHES

CB = Cable Back. To work Cable Back, slip next 2 sts onto cable needle and hold in BACK of work, K2, K2 from cable needle: CB made.

TL = Twist Left. To work Twist Left, slip next 2 sts onto cable needle and hold in FRONT of work, P2, K2 from cable needle: TL made.

TR = Twist Right. To work Twist Right, slip next 2 sts onto cable needle and hold in BACK of work, K2, P2 from cable needle: TR made

PC = Popcorn. To work Popcorn: (P1, K1) twice in next st; sl 2nd, 3rd and 4th st on right hand needle over first st: PC made.

CT = Cable Twist. To work Cable Twist: sl next 3 sts to cable needle, hold in back, K3, K3 from cable needle. Slip next 3 stitches to cable needle, hold in front, K3, K3 from cable needle: cable twist made.

Note: Always slip stitches as to knit; keep yarn in back of slipped stitch.

Instructions

BACK

With smaller straight needles, cast on 92 sts.

Row 1: * Kl tbl, P1; rep from * to end of row.

Rows 2 through 8: Rep row 1.

Change to larger needles and begin pattern.

Row 1 (right side)**:** K1, P1, sl 1, P1, K12; (P1, sl 1) twice, P2; (K2, P8, CB, P8, K2) twice; P2, (sl 1, P1) twice; K12, P1, sl 1, P1, K1.

Row 2: K2, P1, K1, P12, (K1, P1) twice, K2; (P2, K8, P4, K8, P2) twice. K2, (P1, K1) twice, P12, K1, P1, K2.

Row 3: K1, P1, sl 1, P1, K12, (P1, sl 1) twice, P2. (TL, P4, TR, TL, P4, TR) twice, P2, (sl 1, P1) twice, K12, P1, sl 1, P1, K1.

Row 4: K2, P1, K1, P12, (K1, P1) twice, K4, (P2, K4) 8 times, (P1, K1) twice, P12, K1, P1, K2.

Row 5: K1, P1, sl 1, P1, K12, (P1, sl 1) twice, P4, (TL, TR, P4) 4 times, (sl 1, P1) twice, K12, P1, sl 1, P1, K1.

Row 6: K2, P1, K1, P12, (K1, P1) twice, K6, (P4, K8) 3 times, P4, K6, (P1, K1) twice, P12, K1, P1, K2.

Row 7: K1, P1, sl 1, P1, CT over next 12 sts, (P1, sl 1) twice, P6, * CB, P3, (PC) twice, P3 *. Rep from * to * twice more. CB, P6, (sl 1, P1) twice, CT over next 12 sts, P1, sl 1, P1, K1.

Row 8: K2, P1, K1, P12 (K1, P1) twice, K6 (P4, K8) 3 times. P4, K6, (P1, K1) twice, P12, K1, P1, K2.

Row 9: K1, P1, sl 1, P1, K12, (P1, sl 1) twice, P4, (TR, TL, P4) 4 times. (sl 1, P1) twice, K12, P1, sl 1, P1, K1.

Row 10: K2, P1, K1, P12 (K1, P1) twice, K4 (P2, K4) 8 times. (P1, K1) twice, P12, K1, P1, K2.

Row 11: K1, P1, Sl 1, P1, K12, (P1, sl 1) twice. P2, (TR, P4, TL) 4 times, P2, (sl, P1) twice, K12, P1, sl 1, P1, K1.

Row 12: K2, P1, K1, P12 (K1, P1) twice. K2, P2 (K8, P4) 3 times, K8, P2, K2 (P1, K1) twice. P12, K1, P1, K2.

Row 13: K1, P1, sl1, P1, K12, (P1, sl 1) twice, P2, K2, * P3 (PC) twice, P3, CB *;

rep from * to * twice. P3, (PC) twice, P3, K2, P2 (sl 1, P1) twice, K12, P1, sl 1, P1, K1.

Rep Rows 2 through 13 until back measures about 9" from cast-on edge, ending by working a wrong-side row.

RAGLAN SHAPING

Note: *Maintain established pattern throughout.*

Rows 1: Bind off 3 sts at beg of row. Work rem of row in established pattern: 89 sts

Row 2: Rep Row 1: (86 sts).

Row 3: K1, sl 1, PSSO. Work in established pattern to last 3 sts. K2 tog, K1: 84 sts.

Row 4: Work in established pattern.

Rep rows 3 and 4, 21 more times. Sl rem 42 sts onto st holder. Cut yarn.

FRONT
Work same as Back to Raglan Shaping.

RAGLAN SHAPING
Maintaining established pattern,

Row 1: Bind off 3 stitches at beginning of row: 89 sts.

Row 2: Bind off 3 stitches at beginning of row: 86 sts.

Row 3: K1, sl 1, PSSO. Work in pattern to last 3 stitches. K2 tog. K1: 84 sts.

Row 4: Work in established pattern.

Rep Rows 3 and 4, 12 more times. Then rep Row 3 once more: 58 sts.

continued on page 62

BABY FISHERMAN

continued

NECK SHAPING

Both sides of neck are worked at the same time, using separate yarn for each side.

Row 1: Work 15 sts in established pattern for Left Shoulder; sl 28 sts onto a holder for Center Front; with second yarn, work 15 sts in established pattern for Right Shoulder.

Row 2: K1, sl 1, K1, PSSO. Work in est pattern across to within 3 sts of neck edge. K2 tog, K1.

With second yarn, sl 1, K1, PSSO; work in pattern across to last 3 sts, K2 tog, K1: l3 sts on each side.

Row 3: Work in pattern to within 2 sts of neck edge. K2 tog; with second yarn, K2 tog, work across in pattern: 12 sts each side.

Row 4: K1, sl 1, K1, PSSO. Work in pattern across to within three sts of neck edge K2 tog. K1. With second yarn, sl 1, K1, PSSO , work across to last 3 sts. K2 tog. K1: 10 sts each side

Row 5: Work in pattern across row; with second yarn, work in patt across row.

Rows 6 through 9: Rep rows 4 and 5 twice more: 6 sts each side.

Row 10: K1, sl 1, K1, PSSO, K1, K2 tog. With second yarn, sl 1, k1, PSSO, K1, K2tog, K1: 4 sts each side.

Row 11: Purl with separate skeins.

Row 12: Sl 1, K 1, PSSO, K 2 tog; with second yarn, sl 1, K 1, PSSO, K 2 tog: 2 sts each side.

Row 13: P2 tog, cut yarn and pull through. With second yarn, P2 tog, cut yarn and pull through.

SLEEVES (make 2)

With smaller size needles, cast on 56 stitches.

RIBBING

Row 1: * K1 through back loop, P1; repeat from * across.

Row 2: Rep row 1.

Rep rows 1 and 2 eleven times, increasing 16 stitches evenly spaced across last row: 72 sts.

BODY OF SLEEVE

Change to larger needles.

Row 1 (wrong side)**:** (K 2, P 12) 5 times. K2.

Row 2 (right side)**:** (P2, K12) 5 times. P2.

Row 3: Rep Row 1

Row 4: Rep Row 2.

Row 5: Inc in first stitch, K1, (P12, K2) 4 times, P12, K1, inc in last st: 74 sts.

Row 6: P3, (CT, P2) 4 times, CT, P3.

Row 7 (wrong side)**:** Knit previously purled stitches at beg of row, then (P12, K2) 4 times, P12. Knit rem previously purled sts.

Row 8: Purl previous knitted stitches (K12, P2) 4 times, K12. Purl previously knitted sts.

Rep Rows 7 and 8. Working Cable Twist over 12 knit stitches every 12 rows, starting with Row 6. Maintaining pattern and starting with Row 5, inc one stitch at each edge, every fourth row 4 times, then inc every sixth row 3 times. Working new stitches in reverse stockinette stitches (knit the knit stitches on the wrong side and purl the purl stitches on the right side): 86 sts.

Work even, maintaining established pattern for 67 rows. until sleeve measures approximately 10" from cast-on edge. End by working a wrong side row.

Raglan Shaping: Maintain established pattern throughout.

Row 1: Bind off 3 stitches at the beginning of row: 83 sts.

Row 2: Rep Row 1: 80 sts

Row 3: K1, sl 1 , K1, PSSO. Work to last 3 sts. K2 tog, K1: 78 sts.

Row 4: Work across in pattern.

Rep Rows 3 and 4, 25 times more. Place rem 28 stitches onto stitch holder. Cut yarn.

FINISHING

Step 1: Hold one sleeve and back with right sides tog and armhole shaping at top. With tapestry needle and yarn, and carefully matching rows, sew together along armhole edge.

Step 2: Sew same sleeve and front tog in same manner.

Repeat Steps 1 and 2 for other sleeve.

Step 3: Sew sleeve and side seams.

NECK RIBBING

With right side facing and using circular needle, pick up and knit 13 sts along left neck edge, knit 28 sts from front st holder, pick up and knit 13 sts along right neck edge; knit 28 sts from sleeve st holder. knit 42 sts from back st holder, knit 28 sts from sleeve st holder: 152 sts; join.

Place marker to denote rounds

Round 1: * K1 tbl, P1; rep from * around.

Rep Rnd 1 until neck ribbing measures 2".

Bind of all sts loosely in ribbing.

Fold neck ribbing to wrong side and sew loosely in place.

FOR A SPECIAL BABY ON A SPECIAL DAY

Size:
40" x 54"

MATERIALS
Baby-weight yarn,
  14 ozs white
36" Size 10 (6 mm) circular knitting
  needles (or size required for gauge)
Size F (3.75 mm) crochet hook

GAUGE
10 sts = 2" in knitting patt

INSTRUCTIONS

BODY

Cast on 201 sts; do not join, work back and forth in rows.

Row 1 (Right side)**:** Knit..

Row 2: K1; * P9, K1. Rep from * across.

Row 3: P1; * K3, YO; sl 1 as to knit, K2 tog, PSSO, YO, K3, P1. Rep from * across.

Row 4: Purl, working each YO as a st throughout.

Row 5: K1; * YO, K3, sl 1 as to knit, K2 tog, PSSO, K3, YO, K1. Rep from* across.

Row 6: Purl.

Row 7: P1; * K1, YO, K2, sl 1 as to knit, K2 tog, PSSO, K2, YO, K1, P1. Rep from * across.

Row 8: Rep row 2.

Row 9: P1; * K2,YO, K1; sl 1 as to knit, K2 tog, PSSO; K1, YO; K2, P1. Rep from * across.

Rep rows 2 though 9 until piece measures about 38″ long. Then Rep rows 2 and 3 once more. BO all sts loosely. Weave in ends.

BORDER

Hold afghan with right side facing and last row at top. With crochet hook, join yarn in upper left outer corner.

Rnd 1: 3 sc in corner; sc around entire afghan, working 3 sc in each corner sp. Adjust placement of sts as needed to keep work flat. At end of rnd, join in first sc, sl st into next sc.

Rnd 2: Sc in each sc, working 3 sc in center sc of each 3 sc corner group; join.

Rnd 3: Ch 1, sc in joining, ch 3, sk 3 sc, sc in next sc; * ch 3, sk 3 sc, sc in next sc; rep from * around, join.

Rnd 4: Ch 1,* sc in next sc; in next ch-3 sp work (hdc, dc, ch 2, dc, hdc); rep from * around, join.

Rnd 5: Ch 1; * sc in next sc, ch 3, in next ch-2 sp work (sc, ch 2, sc) ch 3; rep from * around, join.

Rnd 6: Ch 1, sc in next sc, ch 3 * 4 dc in next ch-3 sp, ch 1; 3 dc in next ch-2 sp, ch 1, 4 dc in next ch-3 sp; rep from * around, join.

Rnd 7: Ch 4, dc in next dc; * ch 1, dc in next dc; rep from * around, join, finish off.

Weave in ends.

WHITE IS RIGHT

Designed by Susie Adams Steele

Sizes:

	Small 12 months	Medium 18 months	Large 24 months
Finished Garment Chest Measurement:	23"	24"	25"
Finished Garment Waist Measurement (relaxed):	20"	21"	22"

Note: Instructions are written for size small; changes for larger sizes are in parentheses.

MATERIALS

Worsted weight yarn,
  350 (400, 450) grams white
*Note: Photographed model was made
  with Crystal Palace Shimmer, #1736*
14" Size 9 (5.5 mm) knitting needles
  (or size required for gauge)
24" Size 9 (5.5 mm) circular knitting
  needle
24" Size 7 (4.5 mm) circular knitting
  needle
Size F (3.75 mm) crochet hook
Size 16 tapestry needle
Stitch holder
Six ³⁄₈" white buttons with shanks
One yard ³⁄₄"wide flat elastic
Sewing needle and matching thread

GAUGE

9 sts = 2" in stockinette st
  (knit one row, purl one row)

SPECIAL STITCH

SSK: Slip, Slip, Knit
Slip 2 sts as to knit, one at a time; insert
tip of left-hand needle through front of
slipped sts from left to right; knit
together: SSK made.

Blouse Instructions

BACK

Starting at lower edge with straight
needles, cast on 51 (55, 59) sts.

Row 1 (wrong side)**:** Knit.

Row 2: Knit.

Row 3: Purl.

Row 4: K1; * YO, SSK (see Special
Stitch); rep from * across.

Row 5: Purl.

Row 6: * SSK; YO, rep from * to last
st, K1.

Rows 7 through 10: Rep Rows 3
through 6.

Row 11: Knit.

BODY

Row 1 (right side)**:** Knit.

Row 2: Purl.

Rep Rows 1 and 2 until piece measures
7 ¹⁄₂" (8", 8") from cast-on edge, ending by working a wrong-side row.

SLEEVES

Row 1 (right side)**:** Cast on 6 (8, 8) sts
for right sleeve back; knit across: 57
(63, 67) sts.

Row 2: For left back sleeve: Cast on 6 (8, 8) sts for left sleeve back; purl across: 63 (71, 75) sts.

Row 3: Knit.

Row 4: Purl.

Rep Rows 3 and 4 until sleeves measure 4 ½" (5", 5") from cast-on rows, ending by working a wrong-side row.

Bind off. Mark center 23 sts for neckline.

FRONT

Work same as back to sleeves.

SLEEVES

Row 1 (right side)**:** Cast on 6 (8, 8) sts for left sleeve front; knit across: 57 (63, 67) sts.

Row 2: Cast on 6 (8, 8) sts for right sleeve front; purl across: 63 (71, 75) sts.

Row 3: Knit.

Row 4: Purl.

Rep Rows 3 and 4 until sleeves measure 2 ½" (3", 3"), ending by working a wrong-side row.

RIGHT SHOULDER AND NECKLINE SHAPING

Row 1 (right side)**:** Knit 26 (30, 30) and place on stitch holder for left shoulder; bind off center 11 (11, 15) sts for front neck. Knit rem 26 (30, 30) sts.

continued on page 68

WHITE IS RIGHT

continued

Row 2: Purl.

Row 3: For Right Shoulder, bind off 2 sts at neck edge; knit across: 24 (28, 28) sts.

Row 4: Purl.

Rows 5 and 6: Rep Rows 3 and 4. At end of Row 6: 22 (26, 26) sts.

Row 7: K2 tog; knit across: 21 (25, 25) sts.

Row 8: Purl

Rows 9 and 10: Rep Rows 7 and 8. At end of Row 10: 20 (24, 24) sts.

Work even in stockinette stitch until shoulder measures same as back.

Bind off.

LEFT SHOULDER AND NECKLINE SHAPING

Place sts from stitch holder onto one needle; with wrong side facing, join yarn at neck edge.

Row 1 (wrong side)**:** Bind off 2 sts; purl across: 24 (28, 28) sts.

Row 2 (right side)**:** Knit.

Rows 3 and 4: Rep Rows 1 and 2. At end of Row 4: 22 (26, 26) sts.

Row 5: P2 tog; purl across: 21 (25, 25) sts.

Row 6: Knit.

Row 7: Rep Row 5: 20 (24, 24) sts.

Work even in stock st until shoulder measures same as back.

Bind off.

FINISHING

Sew underarm and side seams. Do not sew shoulder seams.

EDGING

With right side of back facing, use crochet hook to join yarn at base of right sleeve edge in side of Row 1 to left of right underarm seam; ch 1, sc in same sp and in side of every other row to next corner; 3 sc in corner; sc in each st across back; 3 sc in corner in side of every other row to left underarm seam, and in side of every other row along front edge of left sleeve; 3 sc in next corner; working along left front shoulder, sc in next 9 (11, 11) sts; * ch 8, sl st in same st: button loop made; sc in next 5 (6, 6) sts * rep from * once, make button loop in next st; 3 sc in next corner; working along front neckline, sc in side of every other row to center front; in each st across front; and in side of every other row to next corner; 3 sc in next corner: rep from * to * twice, make one more button loop; sc in each st to next corner; 3 sc in corner; on right sleeve edge, sc in side of every other row to first sc. Join in first sc.

Sew buttons opposite button loops.

Skirt Instructions

LACE BORDER

Starting at lower edge with larger size circular needle, cast on 153 (165, 177) sts. Do not join; work back and forth in rows.

Rows 1 and 2: Knit.

Row 3 (wrong side)**:** Purl.

Row 4: K1; * YO, SSK (see Special Stitch); rep from * across.

Row 5: Purl.

Row 6: * SSK; YO, rep from * to last st; K1.

Rows 7 through 10: Rep Rows 3 through 6.

Row 11: Knit.

BODY

Row 1 (right side)**:** Knit.

Row 2: Purl.

Rows 3 through 10: Rep Rows 1 and 2.

Row 11 (decrease row)**:** K1 (5, 9); * SSK; K17 (14, 12); rep from * 7 (9, 11) times more: 145 (155, 165) sts.

Row 12: Purl.

Rows 13 through 20: Rep Rows 1 and 2.

Row 21 (decrease row)**:** K1 (5, 9); * SSK; K16 (13, 11); rep from * 7 (9, 11) times more: 137 (145, 153) sts.

Rep Rows 1 and 2 until piece measures about 7" (7 1/2", 8") from cast-on edge.

WAISTBAND

Change to smaller size circular needles. Do not join; work back and forth in rows.

Row 1 (right side)**:** K9 (1, 1); * SSK; K6 (6; 6); rep from * 15 (17, 18) times more: 121 (127, 134) sts.

Row 2: Purl.

Row 3: Knit.

Rows 4 through 7: Rep Rows 2 and 3 twice.

Rows 8 (turning row) **and 9:** Knit.

Rows 10 through 15: Rep Rows 2 and 3 three times.

Row 16: Knit.

Bind off loosely.

FINISHING

Step 1: Turn 1 inch of waistband to wrong side. Using sewing needle and matching thread, sew to back of skirt forming a channel for the elastic. Do not close ends.

Step 2: Sew side seam from lower edge to waistband.

Step 3: Cut elastic 1" shorter than waist measurement; run elastic through waistband channel. Sew ends of elastic together. Slip stitch ends of channel together.

PRECIOUS PARKA

Sizes:	24 months	36 months
Finished Garment Chest Circumference:	28″	30″

Note: *Instructions are written for size 24 months; changes for size 36 months are in parentheses.*

MATERIALS
Sport weight yarn,
  10 oz red
Eyelash yarn,
  15 oz red

Note: *Photographed model was made with Lion Brand Babysoft, Color #113 Red, and Lion Brand Fun Fur, Color #113 Red.*

14″ Size 10 (6 mm) straight knitting needles (or size required for gauge)
Tapestry needle

GAUGE
4 sts = 1″ with sport weight and eyelash yarn held together in garter st (knit every row)

Instructions
Note: *Throughout pattern, work with one strand of sport weight and one strand of eyelash held together.*

BACK
Cast on 56 (60) sts.

Work in garter st (knit every row) until piece measures 14″ (15″).

Bind off.

FRONT
Cast on 56 (60) sts.

Work in garter st until piece measures 12″ (13″) from cast-on row.

Dividing Row: Knit 18 (20) sts; add new yarns and bind off 20 sts, knit rem 18 (20) sts.

Working each side with separate balls of yarn, bind off one st at each neck edge every 4 rows 4 times: 14 (16) sts rem on each side. Continue working on rem sts until front measures the same as back. Bind off all stitches.

SLEEVES (make 2)
Cast on 32 sts.

Work in garter st, increasing one st at each end of needle every 4 rows 9 (10) times: 50 (52) sts. Work even until sleeve measures 9″ (10″) from cast-on edge. Bind off.

HOOD

Cast on 32 sts.

Work in garter st until hood measures 20" (21") from cast on edge. Bind off.

FINISHING

With the sport yarn only threaded into tapestry needle, sew shoulder seams. Sew sleeves into armholes and sew sleeve and side seams. Fold hood in half along long side and sew tog. Sew each side of hood in place on sweater, starting at front and working across to center back, stretching hood to fit neck edge.

Weave in loose ends.

LITTLE FASHIONISTA

Designed by Sandy Scoville

Vest Sizes:

	12 months	18 months	24 months
Finished Garment Chest Measurement:	24"	25"	26"

Note: *Instructions are written for size 12 months; changes for larger sizes are in parentheses.*

Hat Size:

19" circumference head

MATERIALS

Novelty "fur" yarn,
  1 ½ oz white (all sizes)
Worsted weight yarn,
  10 (11, 12) oz blue denim
Note: *Photographed model was made with Adriafil A&S Stars, Color #80 White and Red Heart® Plush™, Color #9823 French Blue*
29" Size 10½ (6.5 mm) circular knitting needle (or size required for gauge)

16" size 8 (5 mm) circular knitting
  needle
2 large stitch holders
Size 16 tapestry needle

GAUGE

14 sts = 4" with larger size needle and
  2 strands of worsted weight yarn
  held together in stockinette st (knit
  one row, purl one row)

Vest Instructions

Note: *Slip all sts as to knit.*

BODY

Beginning at lower edge with larger size needles and 2 strands of blue, cast on 80 (86, 90) sts; do not join, work back and forth in rows.

Row 1 (right side): Knit.

Row 2: Purl. Rep Rows 1 and 2 until piece measures 7" (7", 8").

DIVIDING ROW

Row 1 (right side): Sl 1, K1, PSSO; K16 (17, 18); these sts form right front; bind off 4 (5, 5) sts for right underarm; K36 (38, 40) for back; bind off 4 (5, 5) sts for left underarm; for left front, K16 (17, 18), K2 tog: 70 (74, 78) sts.

Row 2: Purl to first underarm; slip back and right front stitches onto stitch holders.

LEFT FRONT SHOULDER AND NECKLINE SHAPING

Row 1 (right side): Sl 1, K1, PSSO; knit to last 2 sts, K2 tog: 15 (16, 17) sts.

Row 2: Purl.

Row 3: Knit to last 2 sts, K2 tog: 14 (15, 16) sts.

Row 4: Purl.

Rows 5 through 14 (14, 16): Rep Rows 3 and 4. At end of Row 14 (14, 16): 9 (10, 10) sts.

Work even in stock st until armhole measures 4"(5", 5"), ending by working a right-side row. Bind off.

BACK SHOULDER SHAPING

Move back stitches from stitch holder onto left-hand needle; hold with wrong side facing you. Join 2 strands of blue.

Row 1 (wrong side)**:** Purl.

Row 2 (right side)**:** Sl 1, K1, PSSO; knit to last 2 sts, K2 tog: 34 (36, 38) sts.

Row 3: Purl.

Work even in stock st until armhole measures 1 row less than left front.

NECKLINE SHAPING

Row 1 (right side)**:** For right back shoulder: K8 (9, 9), K2 tog;

For neckline: bind off next 14 (14, 16) sts.

For left back shoulder: K1, pass st on needle over K1; K8 (9, 9).

Bind off left back shoulder sts; join 2 strands of blue, bind off right back shoulder sts.

continued on page 74

LITTLE FASHIONISTA
continued

RIGHT FRONT SHOULDER AND NECKLINE SHAPING

Move right front shoulder sts from stitch holder onto needle, hold with wrong side facing.

Row 1 (wrong side)**:** Purl.

Row 2 (right side)**:** Sl 1, K1, PSSO; knit to last 2 sts, K2 tog: 15 (16, 17) sts.

Row 3: Purl.

Row 4: Sl 1, K1, PSSO, knit across: 14 (15, 16) sts.

Row 5: Purl.

Row 6: Rep Row 4.

Rows 7 through 14 (14, 16): Rep Rows 5 and 6. At end of Row 14 (14, 16): 9 (10, 10) sts.

Work even in stock st until armhole measures same as left front.

Bind off. Sew shoulder seams.

TRIM
Lower Edge Trim
Hold vest with right side facing you and lower edge at top.

Row 1 (right side)**:** With larger size needles and white, pick up and knit one st in each cast-on st along lower edge.

Row 2: Knit.

Row 3: Purl.

Row 4: Knit.

Bind off as to purl.

Armhole Trim
Note: *Armhole trim is worked in rnds. Do not turn.*

Hold vest with right side facing you.

Rnd 1 (right side)**:** Beginning at one underarm with smaller size needles and white, pick up and knit one st in each bound-off st, one st in side of each row to shoulder seam; one st in seam, one st in side of each row to first st. Do not turn.

Rnds 2 through 4: Purl.

Bind off as to purl.

Work other armhole trim in same manner.

Neckline Trim
Hold vest with right side facing you and right front at top.

Row 1 (right side)**:** Beginning at first row of right front neckline shaping, with larger size needle and white, pick up and knit one st in side of each row to shoulder seam, in seam, in side of next row on back, in each bound-off st along back neckline, in side of next row on back, in next seam, and in side of each row along left front neckline shaping.

Row 2: Sl 1, K1, PSSO; knit to last 2 sts, K2 tog.

Row 3: P2 tog tbl; purl to last 2 sts, P2 tog.

Row 4: Rep Row 2.

Bind off as to purl.

Hat Instructions
Starting at lower edge, with larger size needle and 2 stands of worsted weight held together, cast on 66 sts; do not join, work back and forth in rows.

Row 1 (right side)**:** Knit.

Row 2: Purl.

Rep Rows 1 and 2 until piece measures about 4″ from beg, ending by working a Row 2.

CROWN

Row 1 (right side)**:** * K2 tog, K1; rep from * across: 44 sts.

Row 2: Purl.

Row 3: K2 tog; * K1, K2 tog; rep from * across: 29 sts.

Row 4: Purl.

Row 5: Rep Row 3. At end of row: 19 sts.

Row 6: Purl.

Row 7: K1, (K2 tog) 9 times: 10 sts.

Cut yarn, leaving a 18″ end. Insert end into tapestry needle; draw through rem sts on needle; remove needle. Leave long end for sewing.

CUFF

Hold hat with wrong side facing you and cast-on edge at top.

Row 1 (wrong side)**:** With larger size needle and white, pick up and knit one st in each cast-on st: 66 sts.

Row 2 (right side)**:** Purl.

Row 3: Knit.

Rows 4 through 13: Rep Rows 2 and 3 five times.

Row 14: Purl.

Bind off as to knit, leaving a 12″ end for sewing.

FINISHING

Step 1: At top of crown, draw yarn end tight to bring sts together. With wrong sides facing, sew back seam, carefully matching rows and colors. Turn right-side out.

Step 2: Fold cuff up so right side is facing.

75

ALL DRESSED UP

Designed by Sandy Scoville

Sizes:	12 months	18 months	24 months
Body Chest Measurements:	18"	20"	22"
Finished Chest Measurement:	20"	22"	24"

Note: *Instructions are written for size 12 months; changes for larger sizes are in parentheses.*

MATERIALS

Sport weight cotton yarn,
  9 (10, 11) oz yellow

Note: *Photographed model was made with Patons® Grace, Color #60603 Apricot*

14" Size 4 (3.5 mm) knitting needles (or size required for gauge)

16" Size 4 (3.5 mm) circular knitting needle

Small stitch holder

Size 16 tapestry needle

2 ½" length white narrow Velcro®

1 yd ¼" ribbon to match yarn

Ten 1"wide pre-made ribbon flowers with leaves

Two ¼" wide ribbon flowers with leaves

1 yd 2" wide gathered eyelet lace, cream

Sewing needle and matching thread

GAUGE

13 sts = 2" in stockinette st (knit one row, purl one row)

Instructions

BACK

Skirt

Starting at back, for First Point:

Cast on 3 sts.

Row 1 (right side): Knit.

Row 2: Inc (to inc, knit in front and in back of st), K1, inc: 5 sts.

Row 3: K2, K1 in next st on row below, K2.

Row 4: Inc; knit to last st; inc: 7 sts.

Row 5: K2; * K1 in next st on row below, K1; rep from * once more; K1.

Row 6: Rep Row 4: 9 sts.

Row 7: K2; * K1 in next st on row below, K1; rep from * to last st; K1.

Row 8: Rep Row 4: 11 sts.

Rows 9 through 16: Rep Rows 7 and 8. At end of Row 16: 19 sts.

Cut yarn.

Second to Fifth Points

On same needle, cast on 3 sts.

Rows 1 through 16: Rep Rows 1 through 16 of first point.

Rep for other points.

At end of fifth point: 95 sts on needle.

BODY

Row 1 (right side): Knit across all points.

Row 2: Knit.

Decrease Row (wrong side): K1 (3, 3); * K2 tog; K2 (3, 4); rep from * 22 (17, 14) times more; K2 tog: 71 (76, 79) sts.

BODICE

Row 1 (right side): Knit.

Row 2: Purl.

For Sizes 12 Months and 24 Months Only:

Row 3 (eyelet row): * K2 tog; YO; rep from * to last st; K1.

For Size 18 Months Only:

Row 3 (eyelet row): K1; * YO, K2 tog; rep from * to last st; K1.

For All Sizes:

Row 4: Purl.

Rows 5 through 7: Knit.

Row 8: Purl.

Rows 9 and 10: Rep Rows 7 and 8.

LEFT BACK ARMHOLE AND SHOULDER SHAPING

Row 1 (right side): Bind off 5 (4, 3) sts; K28 (31, 34), slip these sts onto stitch holder for right back; bind off 5 (6, 5) sts for center back opening; K33 (35, 37).

Row 2: Bind off 5 (4, 3) sts; P 28 (31, 34) sts.

Row 3: Knit.

Row 4: Purl.

Rep Rows 3 and 4 until armhole measures 3″ (3″, 3 1/2″), ending by working a wrong-side row.

LEFT BACK NECKLINE SHAPING

Row 1: Bind off 11 (12, 13) sts; knit across: 17 (19, 21) sts.

Row 2: Purl.

Row 3: K2 tog tbl; knit across: 16 (18, 20) sts.

Rows 4 through 7 (9, 9): Rep Rows 2 and 3 twice (3, 3). At end of Row 7 (9, 9): 14 (15, 17) sts.

Bind off.

RIGHT BACK ARMHOLE AND SHOULDER SHAPING

Slip sts from holder onto needle.

front

back

Row 3: K2, * K1 in next st on row below; K1; rep from * to last st; K1.

Row 4: Knit.

Row 5: K1; * K1 in next st on row below; K1; rep from * across.

Row 6: Knit.

Rep Rows 3 through 6 until piece measures 7 1/2″ (7 1/2″, 8 1/2″) from Body Row 1, ending by working a right-side row.

continued on page 78

ALL DRESSED UP
continued

Row 1 (wrong side)**:** Purl.

Row 2 (right side)**:** Knit

Rep Rows 1 and 2 until armhole measures 3" (3", 3½"), ending by working a right-side row.

RIGHT BACK NECKLINE SHAPING

Row 1 (wrong side)**:** Bind off 11 (12, 13) sts; purl across: 17 (19, 21) sts.

Row 2 (right side)**:** Knit to last 2 sts; K2 tog: 16 (18, 20) sts.

Row 3: Purl.

Rows 4 through 7 (9, 9): Rep Rows 2 and 3 twice (3, 3). At end of Row 7 (9, 9): 14 (15, 17) sts.

Bind off.

LEFT CENTER BACK PLACKET

Row 1 (right side)**:** Hold back with right side of left back bodice facing; pick up and knit 20 (22, 22) sts along one center back edge.

Row 2: Purl.

Row 3: Knit.

Rows 4 and 5: Rep Rows 2 and 3.

Row 6: Purl.

Bind off.

RIGHT CENTER BACK PLACKET

Work same as left center back placket along opposite back edge.

FRONT

Work same as back to armhole and shoulder shaping.

ARMHOLE AND SHOULDER SHAPING

Row 1 (right side)**:** Bind off 5 (4, 3) sts; knit across.

Row 2: Bind off 5 (4, 3) sts; purl across: 61 (68, 73) sts.

Row 3: Knit.

Row 4: Purl.

Rep Rows 3 and 4 until armhole measures 2½" (2½", 3").

RIGHT FRONT NECKLINE SHAPING

Row 1: K19 (21, 23), slip these sts onto stitch holder for left front shoulder; bind off 23 (26, 27) sts; K19 (21, 23).

Row 2: Purl.

Row 3: K2 tog tbl; knit across: 18 (20, 22) sts.

Rows 4 through 11 (13, 13): Rep Rows 2 and 3, 4 (5, 5) times. At end of Row 11 (13, 13): 14 (15, 17) sts.

Work in stock st until right front measures same as back.

Bind off.

LEFT FRONT NECKLINE SHAPING

Slip sts from holder onto needle.

Row 1 (wrong side)**:** Purl.

Row 2: Knit to last 2 sts; K2 tog: 18 (20, 22) sts.

Rows 3 through 10 (12, 12): Rep Rows 1 and 2, 4 (5, 5) times. At end of Row 10 (12, 12): 14 (15, 17) sts.

Work in stock st until left front measures same as back.

Bind off.

Sew shoulder seams.

COLLAR

Row 1 (right side): Beginning at center back to left of left back placket, with 16" circular needle, pick up and knit one st in each bound off st, in end of each row along shoulder to front; one st in each bound-off st along front, 1 st in end of each row along right shoulder, and 1 st in each bound-off st to right back placket, ending with an odd number of sts.

Row 2 (right side): Knit.

Row 3: Inc; knit to last st; inc.

Row 4: K2; * K1 in next st on row below, K1; rep from * to last st; K1.

Rows 5 through 10: Rep Rows 3 and 4.

Bind off.

SLEEVES (make 2)

Cast on 49 sts.

Row 1 (right side): Knit.

Row 2: Purl.

Rows 3 through 6: Rep Rows 1 and 2 twice.

Row 7 (turning row): Purl.

Row 8: Purl.

Rows 9 through 14: Rep Rows 1 and 2.

Rows 15 and 16: Knit.

Row 17: * Inc; K5; rep from * 7 times more; inc: 58 sts.

Row 18: Inc; knit across: 59 sts.

Row 19: K2; * K1 in next st on row below, K1; rep from * to last st; K1.

Row 20: Knit.

Row 21: K1; * K1 in next st on row below, K1; rep from * across.

Row 22: Knit.

Rep Rows 19 through 22 until sleeve measures 3 1/2" from turning row, ending by working a right side row.

For Sizes 12 and 18 Months Only:
Last Row (wrong side): K3; * K2 tog; K6; rep from * 6 times more: 52 sts.

Bind off.

For Size 24 Months Only:
Knit.

Bind off.

Rep for other sleeve.

FINISHING

Step 1: With tapestry needle and yarn, sew sleeves to armholes, easing to fit.

Step 2: Sew underarm and side seams. Hem sleeves, turning under at turning row.

Step 3: Cut Velcro® lengthwise to fit placket opening. Separate; with sewing needle and matching thread, sew to plackets.

Step 4: Thread ribbon into tapestry needle; weave through eyelets, beginning and ending at center front. Tie ribbon into bow.

Step 5: Beginning at center back, sew right side of lace to wrong side of lower edge along joining row behind points.

Step 5: Referring to photo, tack 10 large ribbon flowers along lower edge between points, and one small ribbon flower to each end of ribbon.

REACH FOR THE STARS

Designed by Sandy Scoville

Sizes:

	18 months	24 months	3 years
Body Chest Measurements:	20" - 21"	22" - 23"	24" - 25"
Finished Garment Chest Measurement:	24"	26"	28"

Note: *Instructions are written for size 18 months; changes for larger sizes are in parentheses.*

MATERIALS

Worsted weight chenille yarn,
  6 (7, 8) oz yellow
  1 oz each of teal, dk peach and
  rust (all sizes)
Note: *Photographed model was made with Crystal Palace Cotton Chenille, Colors #1317 Yellow; #2230 Peach; #8166 rust, and #9687 Teal*
14" Size 6 (4 mm) knitting needles
  (or size required for gauge)
Size 16 tapestry needle
Three 3/8" yellow buttons for shoulder
Assorted star buttons
Sewing needle and matching thread

GAUGE

9 sts = 2" in stockinette st
  (knit one row, purl one row)

Instructions

BACK

Starting at lower edge with yellow, cast on 51 (55, 59) sts.

Ribbing

Row 1 (right side): K1; * P1, K1; rep from * across.

Row 2: P1; * K1, P1; rep from * across. Join peach, do not cut yellow.

Rows 3 and 4: Rep Rows 1 and 2. Cut peach.

Rows 5 and 6: With yellow, rep Rows 1 and 2.

Body

Row 1 (right side): Knit; inc (knit in front and back of st) 3 (2, 1) sts evenly spaced across row: 54 (57, 60) sts.

Row 2: Purl.

Row 3: Knit.

Row 4: Purl.

Rep Rows 3 and 4 until piece measures 7 1/2" (7 1/2", 8") from beg.

UNDERARM SHAPING

Row 1 (right side): Bind off first 4 sts; knit across: 50 (53, 56) sts.

Row 2: Bind off first 4 sts; purl across: 46 (49, 52) sts.

Row 3: Knit.

Row 4: Purl.

Rep Rows 3 and 4 until armhole measures 3" (3", 3½").

Top Ribbing

For Size 24 Months Only:

Row 1 (right side): * K1; * P1, K1; rep from * across.

Row 2: P1; * K1, P1; rep from * across. Join peach; do not cut yellow.

Continue with Row 3 below.

For Sizes 24 Months and 3 Years only:

Rows 1 and 2 (right side) : * K1, P1; rep from * across. Join peach; do not cut yellow.

Rows 3 and 4 (all sizes): Rep Rows 1 and 2. At end of Row 4, cut peach.

Rows 5 and 6: With yellow, rep Rows 1 and 2.

Bind off in ribbing first 35 (38, 41) sts; K11. Join peach; cut yellow.

BUTTONHOLE PLACKET

Row 1 (wrong side): With peach, purl.

Row 2: Knit.

Row 3: Purl.

Row 4: K2, YO, K2 tog; * K1, YO, K2 tog; rep from * once more; K1.

Row 5: Purl.

Row 6: Knit.

Row 7: Bind off as to purl.

FRONT

Work same as back to bind-off row.

Bind off all sts in ribbing.

POCKETS

Row 1 (right side): Hold front with right side facing, and working in Row 1 of front body, with rust, pick up and knit

one st in each of first 18 (19, 20) sts; drop rust, join peach, do not cut rust; with peach, pick up and knit one st in each of next 18 (19, 20) sts; drop peach, join teal, do not cut peach; with teal, pick up and knit one st in each of next 18 (19, 20) sts: 54 (57, 60) sts.

Note: *when working pockets, twist strands when changing colors to prevent holes in work.*

Row 2: (Using colors to match Row 1) Purl.

Work in stock st, keeping color sequence, for 16 more rows.

With corresponding colors, bind off all stitches as to purl. Cut all colors, leaving 12" ends for sewing. Sew on decorative buttons. With tapestry needle and matching yarn, with right side facing, sew side edges of pockets to side edges of body. With matching colors, sew vertical seams separating pockets.

SLEEVES (make one with teal stripe and one with rust stripe)

Starting at lower edge with yellow, cast on 26 (26, 28) sts.

Ribbing

Row 1 (right side): * K1, P1; rep from * across.

Row 2: * K1, P1; rep from * across.

Join teal or rust, do not cut yellow.

Rows 3 and 4: Rep Rows 1 and 2. Cut teal or rust.

Rows 5 and 6: With yellow, rep Rows 1 and 2.

Arm

Row 1 (right side): Inc (knit in front and back of st); * K2, inc; rep from * 7 (7, 7) times more; inc: 36 (36, 38) sts.

Row 2: Purl.

Row 3: Knit.

Row 4: Purl.

Rep Rows 3 and 4 until sleeve measures 9½" (9½", 10").

Bind off.

FINISHING

Step 1: Hold front and back with wrong sides tog; fold buttonhole placket over front ribbing and pin to hold; turn with right sides tog; sew along side edge, leaving shoulder open.

Step 2: Sew right shoulder seam. Sew underarm seams. Sew sleeve seams. Sew sleeves to body.

Step 3: Sew 3/8" yellow buttons to front opposite Buttonhole Placket.

TIME TO SUIT UP

Designed by Sandy Scoville

Sizes:

	12 months	18 months	24 months
Body Chest Measurements:	18"	20"	22"
Finished Garment Chest Measurement:	22"	24"	26"

Note: *Instructions are written for size 12 months; changes for larger sizes are in parentheses.*

MATERIALS
Worsted weight yarn,
   5 (5 1/2, 6) oz tan
   5 (5 1/2, 6) cream
Note: *Photographed model was made in TLC® Amoré™, Colors #3103 Vanilla and #3220 Wheat*
24" Size 6 (4 mm) circular knitting
   needle (or size required for gauge)
Small stitch holder
1/2 yd 1/8"wide elastic
Three 3/8" diameter buttons
Size 16 tapestry needle
Sewing needle and matching thread

GAUGE
9 sts = 2" in stockinette st
   (knit one row, purl one row)

Top Instructions
BACK
Ribbing
Starting at lower edge with tan, cast on 53 (57, 61) sts.

Row 1 (right side): * K3, P1; rep from * to last st; K1.

Row 2: Rep Row 1. Join cream; do not cut tan.

Rows 3 and 4: With cream, rep Row 1.

Rows 5 through 8: With tan, rep Row 1. Cut tan.

BODY
Row 1 (right side): With cream, knit.

Row 2: Purl.

Rep Rows 1 and 2 until body measures 6 1/2" (7", 7 1/2").

ARMHOLE SHAPING
Row 1 (right side): Bind off 4 sts; knit across.

Row 2: Bind off 4 sts; purl across: 45 (49, 53) sts.

LEFT BACK SHOULDER SHAPING
Row 1 (right side): K20 (22, 24), slip these sts onto stitch holder for right back shoulder; bind off 5 sts; K20 (22, 24) sts.

Row 2: Purl.

Row 3: Knit.

Row 4: Purl.

Rep Rows 3 and 4 until armhole measures 3" (3", 3 1/2"), ending by working a wrong side row.

LEFT BACK NECKLINE SHAPING
Row 1 (right side): Bind off 7 (8, 8) sts; knit across: 13 (14, 16) sts.

Row 2: Purl.

Row 3: K2 tog tbl; knit across: 12 (13, 15) sts.

Row 4: Purl.

Rows 5 and 6: Row Rep Rows 3 and 4: At end of Row 6: 11 (12, 14) sts.

Continue in stock st until armhole measures 4".

Bind off.

RIGHT BACK SHOULDER SHAPING

Hold back with wrong side facing you; slip sts from holder onto needle.

Row 1 (wrong side)**:** With cream, purl.

Row 2 (right side)**:** Knit.

Row 3: Purl.

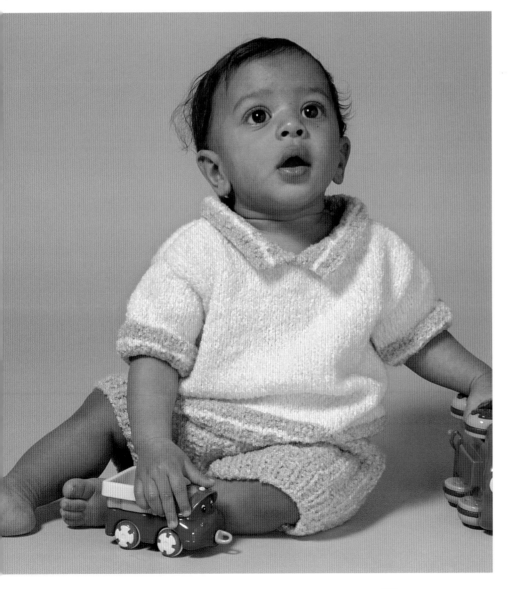

Rep Rows 2 and 3 until armhole measures 3" (3", 3 1/2"), ending by working a wrong-side row.

RIGHT BACK NECKLINE SHAPING

Row 1 (right side)**:** Knit.

Row 2: Bind off 7 (8, 8) sts; purl across: 13 (14, 16) sts.

Row 3: Knit to last 2 sts; K2 tog: 12 (13, 15) sts.

Row 4: Purl.

Rows 5 and 6: Row Rep Rows 3 and 4: 11 (12, 14) sts.

Continue in stock st until right back measures same as left back.

Bind off.

FRONT

Work same as back through Row 2 of armhole shaping.

Continue in stock st until armhole measures 2" (2", 2 1/2"), ending by working a wrong-side row.

RIGHT FRONT NECKLINE SHAPING

Row 1 (right side)**:** K16 (18, 20), place these sts onto stitch holder for left front shoulder; bind off 13 sts for neck; K16 (18, 20).

Row 2: Purl.

Row 3: K2 tog tbl; knit across: 15 (17, 19) sts.

Row 4: Purl.

Rows 5 through 12: Rep Rows 3 and 4, 4 times. At end of Row 12: 11 (13, 15) sts.

For Size 12 Months Only:
Continue in stock st until right front measures same as back. Bind off.

For Sizes 18 and 24 Months Only:
Rows 13 and 14: Rep Rows 3 and 4. At end of Row 4: 12 (14) sts.

Continue in stock st until right front measures same as back. Bind off.

LEFT FRONT NECKLINE SHAPING

Hold front with wrong side facing; slip sts from holder onto needle.

Row 1 (wrong side)**:** Purl

Row 2 (right side)**:** Knit to last 2 sts; K2 tog: 15 (17, 19) sts.

Row 3: Purl.

Rows 4 through 11: Rep Rows 2 and 3, 4 times. At end of Row 12: 11 (13, 15) sts.

83

continued on page 84

TIME TO SUIT UP

continued

For Size 12 Months Only:
Continue in stock st until left front measures same as back.

Bind off.

For Sizes 18 and 24 Months Only:
Rows 12 and 13: Rep Rows 2 and 3. At end of Row 13: 12 (14) sts.

Continue in stock st until left front measures same as back.

Bind off.

Sew shoulder seams.

BUTTONHOLE PLACKET

Row 1 (right side): Hold top with right side of back facing; with tan, pick up and knit 14 (14, 16) sts along right edge of center back opening.

Row 2: Purl.

Row 3: K2 (2, 3); * YO: buttonhole made: K2 tog; K2; rep from * twice more; K0 (0, 1).

Row 4: Purl.

Row 5: Knit.

Bind off.

BUTTON PLACKET

Row 1 (right side): Hold top with right side of back facing; with tan, pick up and knit 14 (14, 16) sts along left back center opening.

Row 2: Purl.

Row 3: Knit.

Rows 4 and 5: Rep Rows 2 and 3.

Bind off.

COLLAR
Right Section

Row 1 (right side): Hold top with wrong side of back facing; beginning at center back in first cream st to right of buttonhole placket, with tan, pick up and knit 29 (29, 33) sts to 7th bound-off st at center front neck edge.

Row 2: * K3, P1; rep from * to last st; K1.

Rows 3 through 5: Rep Row 2. Join cream; do not cut tan.

Rows 6 and 7: With cream, rep Row 2. Cut cream.

Rows 8 and 9: With tan, rep Row 2.

Bind off in patt.

Left Section

Row 1 (right side): Hold top with wrong side of front facing; beginning in same last st of Row 1 of right section at center front, pick up and knit 29 (29, 33) sts to button placket.

Rows 2 through 9: Rep Rows 2 through 9 of right section.

Bind off in patt.

Fold collar to right side.

SLEEVES

Row 1 (right side): Hold top with right side facing and one armhole edge at top; with cream, pick up 37 (37, 41) sts.

Row 2: Purl.

Row 3: Knit.

Row 4: Purl.

Rows 5 and 6: Rep Rows 3 and 4.

Row 7: K2 tog tbl; knit to last 2 sts; K2 tog: 35 (35, 39) sts.

Row 8: Purl.

Rows 9 through 12: Rep Rows 5 through 8. At end of Row 12: 33 (33, 37) sts.

Continue in stock st until sleeve measures 2½ "(2½", 3"), ending by working a wrong side row. Join tan; do not cut cream.

Ribbing

Row 1 (right side): * K3, P1; rep from * to last st; K1.

Rows 2 through 4: Rep Row 1.

Rows 5 and 6: With cream, rep Row 1. At end of Row 6, cut cream.

Rows 7 and 8: With tan, rep Row 1.

Bind off in patt.

Work other sleeve in same manner.

FINISHING

Sew bound-off sts of armhole to top of sleeve edges. Sew sleeve and side seams. Sew buttons opposite buttonholes.

Pants Instrucions

Note: Pants are made in one piece beginning at back waist.

With tan, cast on 49 (53, 57) sts.

RIBBING

Row 1 (right side)**:** K1; * P1, K1; rep from * across.

Row 2: P1; * K1, P1; rep from * across.

Rows 3 through 8: Rep Rows 1 and 2.

BACK BODY

Row 1 (right side)**:** * K3, P1; rep from * to last st; K1.

Rep Row 1 until body measures 6" (6", 7") from end of ribbing, ending by working a wrong-side row.

BACK LEG SHAPING

Row 1 (right side)**:** Bind off 4 sts; work in patt across.

Rep Row 1 until 13 sts remain on needle.

CROTCH

Work in patt until crotch measures 1 ½" (1 ½", 2 ½"), ending by working a wrong-side row.

FRONT BODY

Row 1 (right side)**:** Cast on 4 sts; work in patt across.

Rows 2 through 10: Rep Row 1. At end of row 9 (10, 11): 49 (53, 57) sts.

Next Row: * K3, P1; rep from * to last row; K1.

Rep this last row until front body measures same as back body, ending by working a wrong-side row.

Front Ribbing

Row 1 (right side)**:** K1; * P1, K1; rep from * across.

Row 2: P1; * K1, P1; rep from * across.

Rows 3 through 8: Rep Rows 1 and 2.

Bind off in ribbing.

Leg Ribbing

Row 1 (right side)**:** Hold pants with right side facing and one side edge at top; pick up and knit 43 (45, 49) sts evenly spaced along bound-off edges and crotch to opposite side edge.

Row 2: P1; * K1, P1; rep from * across.

Row 3: K1; * P1, K1; rep from * across.

Rows 4 through 7: Rep Rows 2 and 3.

Bind off in ribbing.

Work other leg ribbing in same manner.

FINISHING

Sew side seams.

Cut elastic 1" shorter than waist measurement.

Thread elastic into tapestry needle; weave through wrong side of waist ribbing, beginning and ending at one side edge. Sew ends tog, overlapping slightly.

BERET

Size:
2 to 4 years

MATERIALS
Eyelash yarn,
  3 ozs white
Note: *Photographed model was made
  with Lion Brand Fun Fur #100 white*
24" Size 6 (4 mm) circular needle
  (or size required for gauge)
8" Size 6 (4 mm) double-pointed
  knitting needles
16" Size 5 (3.75 mm) circular needle

Stitch marker
Tapestry needle

GAUGE
5 sts = 1" with larger size needles
  in stockinette st (knit one row,
  purl one row)

Instructions
With smaller circular needle, cast on 84
sts. Join work, and place marker to
indicate beg of rnds; move marker at
end of each rnd. Work 6 rows of K1,
P1, ribbing. Change to larger circular
needle.

Rnd 1: Inc in first st, K1; * (Inc in each
of next 3 sts, K1) 3 times; inc one st in
next st, K1. Rep from * to last 12 sts,
(inc 1 st in each of next 3 sts, K1) 3
times: 144 sts.

Note: *To increase, knit in front and
back of indicated st.*

Rnd 2: Knit.

Rep Rnd 2 until beret measures 3" from
cast on row.

TOP
Rnd 1: * K16, K2 tog; rep from
* around: 136 sts

Rnd 2 and all even rnds: knit.

Rnd 3: * K15, K2 tog; rep from
* around: 128 sts.

Rnd 5: * K14, K2 tog; rep from
* around: 120 sts.

Rnd 7: * K13, K2 tog; rep from
* around: 112 sts.

Rnd 9: * K12, K2 tog; rep from
* around: 104 sts.

Rnd 11: * K11, K2 tog; rep from
* around: 96 sts.

Rnd 13: * K10, K2 tog; rep from
* around: 88 sts

Note: *When sts can no longer be
accommodated on circular needle,
switch to double-pointed needles and
continue working in rnds.*

Rnd 15: * K9, K2 tog; rep from
* around: 80 sts

Rnd 17: * K8, K2 tog; rep from
* around: 72 sts

16" Size 6 (4 mm) circular needle
(or size required for gauge)

GAUGE

5 sts = 1" in stockinette st
(knit one row, purl one row)

Muff Instructions

Cast on 70 sts. Join work, place marker
to indicate beg of rnd.

Move marker on following rnds.

Rnd 1: Knit.

Rep Rnd 1 until piece measures approximately 6". Bind off. Weave in ends.

Strap Instructions

*Note: Strap is worked from the right
side only. Do not turn. The stitches will
fold toward the wrong side to form a
double-thickness.*

Leaving an 8" end, cast on 3 sts on
circular needle.

Row 1: Knit. Slide sts to opposite end
of needle; do not turn.

Row 2: Carry yarn across wrong side of
sts; knit. Slide sts to the opposite end
of the needle; do not turn.

Rep rows 1 and 2 until the strap
measures the desired length. Bind off,
leaving an 8" end for sewing.

Attach ends of strap to muff so that it
will go around child's neck.

Rnd 19: * K7, K2 tog; rep from
* around: 64 sts

Rnd 21: * K6, K2 tog; rep from
* around: 56 sts

Rnd 23: * K5, K2 tog; rep from
* around: 48 sts

Rnd 25: * K4, K2 tog; rep from
* around: 40 sts

Rnd 27: * K3, K2 tog; rep from
* around: 32 sts

Rnd 29: * K2, K2 tog; rep from
* around: 24 sts

Rnd 31: * K2 tog; rep from
* around: 12 sts

Finish off, leaving a long end.
Thread end into tapestry needle;
draw thread through rem sts and
fasten securely.

MUFF

Size:
Approx 7" x 6"

MATERIALS

Eyelash yarn,
   3 ozs white
Note: *Photographed Model was
   made in Lion Brand Fun Fur Color
   #100 White*

RAINBOW COAT

Designed by Susie Adams Steel

Sizes: 12 months   18 months   24 months

Finished Garment Chest Measurement:	23"	24"	25"

Note: *Instructions are written for size 12 months; changes for larger sizes are in parentheses.*

MATERIALS

Bulky boucle yarn,
   450 (485, 520) yds, variegated
Sport weight yarn,
   1 oz blue
Note: *Photographed model was made with Crystal Palace Musique, Color #9134 Picnic and Bernat® Softee Baby, Color #30184 Baby Denim.*
24" Size 10 (6 mm) circular knitting
   needle (or size required for gauge)
Size G (4 mm) crochet hook
One large stitch holder
Size 16 tapestry needle
Two ⅝" buttons

GAUGE

14 sts = 4" with bulky boucle yarn in
   stockinette st (knit one row, purl
   one row)

Instructions

Note: *Coat is knit in one piece, beginning at lower back edge*

With bulky boucle, cast on 48 (50, 52) sts.

Row 1 (right side)**:** Knit.

Row 2: Purl.

Rep Rows 1 and 2 until piece measures 10½" (11", 11½"), ending by working a wrong side row. Mark row.

SLEEVE SHAPING

Row 1 (right side)**:** Inc in first st (knit in front and back of st); knit to last st, inc in last st: 50 (52, 54) sts.

Row 2: Purl.

Rows 3 through 24: Rep Rows 1 and 2. At end of Row 24: 72 (74, 76) sts.

Row 25: Knit across; cast on 3 sts: 75 (77, 79) sts.

Row 26: Purl across; cast on 3 sts:78 (80, 82) sts.

Rows 27 through 32: Rep Rows 25 and 26. At end of Row 32: 96 (98, 100) sts.

Row 33: Knit across; cast on 3 (7, 9) sts: 99 (105, 109) sts.

Row 34: Purl across; cast on 3 (7, 9) sts: 102 (112, 118) sts.

Row 35: Knit.

Row 36: Purl.

Rep Rows 35 and 36 until sleeves measures 4½" (5", 5½") from Row 34, ending by working a wrong-side row.

SHOULDER SHAPING

Row 1: For right front: K42 (47, 50) sts; place these sts on stitch holder; for neckline, bind off 18 (18, 18) sts; for left front: K42 (47, 50).

Row 2: P42 (47, 50).

LEFT FRONT NECKLINE SHAPING

Row 1 (right side)**:** Knit.

Rows 2, 4, 6, 8, and 10: Purl.

Row 3: Inc; knit across: 43 (48, 51) sts.

Row 5: Rep Row 3: 44 (49, 52) sts.

Row 7: Cast on 2 sts; knit across: 46 (51, 54) sts.

Row 9: Rep Row 7: 48 (53, 56) sts.

Row 11: Cast on 3 sts; knit across: 51 (56, 59) sts.

Rep Rows 1 and 2 for 2" ending by working a right-side row.

LEFT FRONT SLEEVE SHAPING

Row 1 (wrong side)**:** Bind off 3 (7, 9) sts; purl across: 48 (49, 50) sts.

Row 2: Knit.

Row 3: Bind off 3 (3, 3) sts; purl across: 45 (46, 47) sts.

Rows 4 through 9: Rep Rows 2 and 3. At end of Row 8: 36 (37, 38) sts.

Row 10: Knit.

Row 11: Sl 1, P1, PSSO; purl across: 35 (36, 37) sts.

Rows 12 through 33: Rep rows 10 and 11. At end of Row 33: 24 (25, 26) sts. Mark Row 33.

Continue in Stockinette Stitch (knit one row, purl one row) until left front measures 9" (10½", 11") from left front neckline shaping, ending by working a wrong-side row.
Mark row.

89

continued on page 90

RAINBOW COAT
continued

Center Front Curve

Row 1 (right side)**:** Sl 1, K1, PSSO; knit across: 23 (24, 25) sts.

Row 2: Purl.

Row 3: Knit.

Row 4: Purl.

Rows 5 through 28: Rep Rows 1 through 4. At end of Row 28: 17 (18, 19) sts.

Rows 29 and 30: Rep Rows 1 and 2:16 (17, 18) sts.

Rows 31 through 38: Rep Rows 1 through 4 twice. At end of Row 38: 14 (15, 16) sts.

Row 39: Bind off first 2 sts; knit across:12 (13, 14) sts.

Row 40: Purl.

Rows 41 through 44: Rep Rows 39 and 40 twice: 8 (9, 10) sts.

Work even without dec until left front measures same as back from dividing row at shoulder shaping.

Bind off.

RIGHT FRONT NECKLINE SHAPING

Slip sts on holder onto needle and hold with wrong side facing you, P42 (47, 50).

Row 1 (right side)**:** Knit.

Rows 2, 4, 6, 8, and 10: Purl.

Row 3: Knit to last st; inc (knit in front and back of next st: 43 (48, 51) sts.

Row 5: Rep Row 3: 44 (49, 52) sts.

Row 7: Knit across; cast on 2 sts: 46 (51, 54) sts.

Row 9: Rep Row 7: 48 (53, 56) sts.

Row 11: Knit across; cast on 3 sts: 51 (56, 59) sts.

Rep Rows 1 and 2 for 2" until right sleeve measures same as left sleeve to left front sleeve shaping.

Purl one row.

RIGHT FRONT SLEEVE SHAPING

Row 1 (right side)**:** Bind off 3 (7, 9) sts; knit across: 48 (49, 50) sts.

Row 2: Purl.

Row 3: Bind off 3 (3, 3) sts; knit across: 45 (46, 47) sts

Rows 4 through 9: Rep Rows 2 and 3. At end of Row 8: 36 (37, 38) sts.

Row 10: Purl.

Row 11: Sl 1, K1, PSSO; knit across: 35 (36, 37) sts.

Rows 12 through 33: Rep rows 10 and 11. At end of Row 33: 24 (25, 26) sts. Mark Row 32.

Continue in stockinette stitch (knit one row, purl one row) until right front measures 9" (10", 11") from right front neckline shaping, and right front measures same as left front to center front curve at 2nd marked row. Mark this wrong-side row.

CENTER FRONT CURVE

Row 1 (right side)**:** Knit to last 2 sts; K2 tog: 23 (24, 25) sts.

Row 2: Purl.

Row 3: Knit.

Row 4: Purl.

Rows 5 through 28: Rep Rows 1 through 4. At end of Row 28: 17 (18, 19) sts.

Rows 29 and 30: Rep Rows 1 and 2: 16 (17, 18) sts.

Rows 31 through 38: Rep Rows 1 through 4 twice. At end of Row 3:14 (15, 16) sts.

Row 39: Knit.

Row 40: Bind off first 2 sts; purl across: 12 (13, 14) sts.

Rows 41 through 44: Rep Rows Rep Rows 39 and 40 twice: 8 (9, 10) sts.

Work even without dec until right front measures same as left front.

Bind off.

Sew side seams from lower edge to end of each sleeve.

BODY EDGING

Hold coat with right side facing and lower edge at top; with crochet hook, join blue in side seam at edge of left front.

Note: When working around coat edging, it may be necessary to skip rows or add stitches in order to keep edging flat. Crochet loosely.

Rnd 1: Ch 1, sc in same sp, sc in each cast-on st to next seam; sc in seam; sc along bound-off sts along lower front edge, sc in side of each row along center front edge, in next shoulder seam, in each bound-off st across back neckline, in next shoulder seam, in side of each row along center front edge, and in each bound-off st along lower front edge; join in first sc.

Rnds 2 and 3: Ch 1, sc in first sc and in each rem sc; join.

Finish off.

SLEEVE EDGINGS

With crochet hook, join blue in one sleeve seam.

Rnd 1: Ch 1, sc in same sp as joining and in side of each row around; join in first sc.

Rnd 2: Ch 1, sc in same sc and in each rem sc; join.

Finish off.

Repeat for other sleeve edging.

Finish off. Weave in ends.

FINISHING
Button Covers
With crochet hook and blue, ch 2.

Rnd 1: 6 sc in first ch; do not join.

Rnd 2: 2 sc in each sc; do not join: 12 sc.

Rnd 3: (2 sc in next sc, sc in next sc) 6 times:18 sc.

Rnd 4: Sc in each sc.

Rnd 5: Dec over next 2 sc (to work dec: draw up lp in each of next 2 sc, YO and draw through all 3 lps on hook: dec made); sc in next sc; (dec over next 2 sc, sc in next sc) 5 times:12 sc.

Rnd 6: Insert button; working over button, dec 6 times.

Cut yarn, leaving an 8" end. Thread yarn into tapestry needle; weave yarn through rem 6 stitches and draw up tight. Weave in ends.

Button Loop
With crochet hook and blue, ch 18; join to form a ring, being careful not to twist chain. Twist joined ch into a figure 8. Sew through center twist at edge of right front at neckline.

Sew buttons to left and right front edges opposite button loops.

CHRISTENING DRESS & BONNET

Designed by Jodi Lewanda

Size:
Newborn to 3 months
Measurement at underarm: 20"

MATERIALS
Fingering weight yarn,
   175 grams ivory
Note: *Photographed model was made
   with K1,C2 Richesse et Soie, Color
   #9146 Ivory*
14" Size 3 (3.25 mm) straight knitting
   needles (or size required for gauge)
16" Size 3 (3.25 mm) circular knitting
   needle
2 small stitch holders
1 large stitch holder
tapestry needle
3 yds ¼" ribbon
Two ⅜" buttons
Sewing needle and thread to
   match ribbon
Stitch holder
Tapestry needle

GAUGE
13 sts = 2" in Garter Stitch (knit
   every row)

Dress Instructions

YOKE
Note: *Yoke is worked in one piece, beg
at bottom of back.*

With straight needles, cast on 64
stitches.

Rows 1 through 3: Knit.

Row 4 (right side)**:** K32 for right side of
center back.

(Note: *Work is now divided and right
and left sides of yoke are worked with
separate skeins of yarn)*

Join second skein of yarn and knit rem
32 stitches.

Row 5: With first skein of yarn, cast
on 8 sts for sleeve, knit rem 32; with
next skein, K32.

Row 6: Cast on 8 sts for sleeve, knit
rem 32; with next skein, K40: 40 sts
on each side.

Row 7: Continuing to work with two
skeins of yarn, K40 sts each side.

Rep Row 7 until piece measures 3 ¼"
from beg cast-on row, ending by working a wrong-side row.

NECK AND SHOULDER SHAPING

Row 1 (right side)**:** K26, slip rem 14 sts
from this side onto a small stitch holder
for back of neck. With second skein of
yarn K14 and slip these stitches onto a
small stitch holder, knit rem 26 stitches.

FRONT
Working on 26 sts on each side, knit
every row until piece measures 1 ½"
from holders, end by working a wrong-
side row.

Joining row (right side)**:** Working with
one skein of yarn only, K26, cast on 28
sts for center front, knit rem 26 stitches:
80 sts. Cut additional skein of yarn.

Continue knitting each row until the
front measures the same as the back to
cast on stitches for the sleeves, ending
by working a wrong-side row.

Next row: Bind off 8 sts, knit across:
72 sts.

Next row: Bind off 8 sts, knit across: 64 sts.

Knit these 64 sts for 4 more rows. Slip all sts onto a large stitch holder to be worked later for skirt.

NECKBAND

With right side facing, join yarn at left back center top and knit 14 stitches from holder. Pick up and knit 7 sts along left front neck facing, one st in each of the 28 cast-on sts at front of neck, 7 sts along right front neck facing, and 14 sts from other holder: 70 sts.

Work 4 rows of K1, P1 rib. Bind off.

SLEEVEBAND (make 2)

With right side facing, join yarn and pick up 32 sts along one outer sleeve edge.

Work 4 rows of K1, P1 rib. Bind off.

SKIRT

Hold yoke and sleeve section with right side facing and back lower edge across top. With circular needle, join yarn at upper right-hand corner and pick up and knit one st in each of the 64 cast-on sts along back yoke, K64 from holder: 128 sts. Place marker to indicate beg of round.

Join and purl one round. Slip marker on this and every following round.

Note: To increase on next round: With tip of right needle, pull up horizontal bar between sts and knit into the back of it.

Increase Rnd: K1, inc * K2, inc; rep from * to last st, K1: 192 sts.

Rnds 1 and 2: Knit.

Rnd 3: *(K2 tog) twice, (YO, K1) 3 times; YO, (sl 1, K1, PSSO) twice, K1; rep from * across.

Rnd 4: Knit.

Rep Rnds 3 and 4 until skirt measures 26" from underarm, ending by working a Rnd 4.

Purl one round, then bind off.

Sew underarm seams. Weave in all ends.

BUTTON LOOPS

With right side facing, work button loop at top right back center edge as follows: Thread yarn, doubled, into tapestry needle and secure on wrong side. Insert needle again, slightly below first fastening, leaving sufficient sized loop to fit the button. Tack in place. Continue with same yarn and reinforce loop by working buttonhole sts around loop until completely covered. Secure and weave in yarn end. Work a second loop approximately 1" below first, in same manner.

Sew on buttons. Cut two 1-yard lengths of ribbon and hold together. Tie bow at center and tack bow to center front at base of yoke.

93

continued on page 94

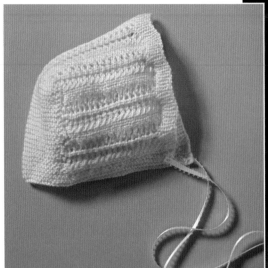

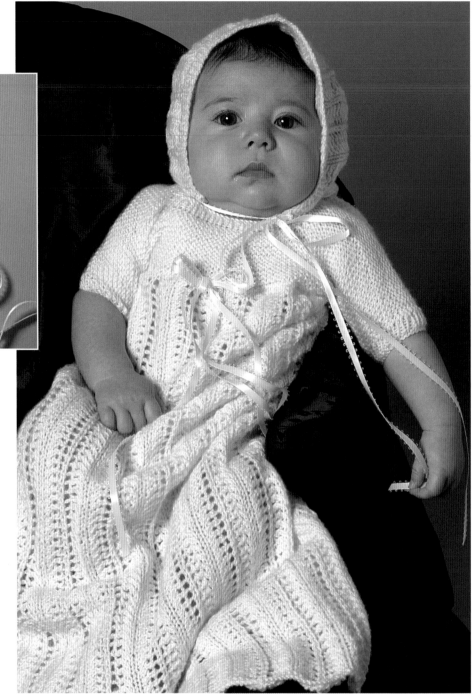

Bonnet Instructions

With straight needles, cast on
99 stitches

BORDER

Rows 1 (right side)**:** K1, * P1, K1;
rep from * across.

Row 2: P1, * K1, P1; rep from * across

Rows 3 through 5: Rep Rows 1 and 2
once more, then rep Row 1 once.

Row 6: Purl.

CROWN

Row 1: K2; *(K2 tog) twice, (YO, K1) 3
times; YO, (sl 1, K1, PSSO) twice, K1;
rep from * to last st, K 1.

Row 2: Purl.

Rep rows 1 and 2 until piece measures
4" from cast on edge, ending by working a purl row. Bind off 30 stitches, knit
the next 39 sts, bind off remaining 30
sts. Cut yarn.

BACK

Join yarn at beginning of row; work rem
39 sts in Garter Stitch (knit every row)

for 2". Continuing in garter stitch,
decrease one stitch at each end every
4th row, 5 times: 29 sts remain; place
sts on holder.

NECKBAND

Hold piece with right side facing.
Starting at bottom of left front edge,
attach yarn and pick up and knit 34 sts,

knit 29 stitches from holder, pick up and
knit 34 stitches from right front edge:
97 sts. Knit 4 rows, bind off.

FINISHING

Sew side seams at back. Cut ribbon in
half and tack one piece to front bonnet
bottom edge on each side.

BABY KIMONO SWEATER

Designed by Susie Adams Steele

Sizes:

	12 months	18 months	24 months
Finished Garment Chest Measurement:	23"	24"	25"

Note: *Instructions are written for size 12 months; changes for larger sizes are in parentheses.*

MATERIALS

Worsted weight yarn,
   4 1/2 (5, 5 1/2) oz green cotton
Chenille yarn,
   1/2 (3/4, 1) oz green
24" Size 8 (5 mm) circular knitting
   needles (or size required for gauge)
24" Size 6 (4 mm) circular knitting
   needles
Size E (3.5 mm) crochet hook
Size 16 tapestry needle
Stitch holder

GAUGE

4 sts = 1" with larger size needles in
stockinette st (knit one row, purl
one row)

Instructions

BACK

Starting at lower edge with larger needles and worsted weight yarn, cast on 52 (54, 56) sts. Do not join; knit back and forth in rows.

Rows 1 through 3: Knit.

Row 4: Purl.

Row 5 (right side)**:** Knit.

Row 6: Purl.

Rep Rows 5 and 6 until piece measures 7" (7 1/2", 8"). Mark last row at both ends for armholes.

Rep Rows 5 and 6 until piece measures 5" (5 1/2", 5 1/2") from marked row.

NECKLINE SHAPING

Row 1 (right side)**:** For right back shoulder, K15 (16, 17), place these sts on stitch holder; for neckline, bind off next 22 sts; for left back shoulder, K15 (16, 17).

LEFT BACK SHOULDER

Row 1 (wrong side)**:** Purl.

Row 2: Knit.

Row 3: Purl.

Bind off.

RIGHT BACK SHOULDER

Slip stitches from stitch holder to needle; hold piece with wrong side facing you; with larger size needle, join worsted weight yarn in first st at neckline edge.

Rows 1 through 3: Rep Rows 1 through 3 of Left Back Shoulder. Bind off.

LEFT FRONT

Starting at lower edge with larger needle and worsted weight, cast on 38 (40, 42) sts.

Rows 1 through 3: Knit.

continued on page 96

BABY KIMONO SWEATER

continued

Row 4: Purl

Row 5 (right side)**:** Knit.

Row 6: Purl.

Rep Rows 5 and 6 until piece measures same as back to armhole marker. Mark both ends of this row for armhole.

NECKLINE SHAPING

Row 1 and all right-side rows: Knit.

Rows 2, 4, 6, 8, 10, 12, 14, and 16: Bind off 2 (2, 2) sts; purl across. At end of Row 16: 22 (24, 26) sts.

Row 18: Bind off 1 (2, 2) sts; purl across: 21 (22, 24) sts.

Row 20: Bind off 1 (1, 2) sts; purl across: 20 (21, 22) sts.

Rows 22, 24, 26, 28, and 30: Bind off 1 (1, 1) st: purl across: 15 (16, 17) sts.

Work in stockinette stitch until left front measures same as back. Bind off.

RIGHT FRONT

Starting at lower edge with larger size needle and worsted weight, cast on 38 (40, 42) sts.

Rows 1 through 3: Knit.

Row 4: Purl.

Row 5: Knit.

Row 6: Purl.

Rep Rows 5 and 6 until piece measures same as back to armhole marker. Mark both ends of this row for armhole.

NECKLINE SHAPING

Row 1 (right side)**:** Bind off 2 (2, 2) sts; knit across: 36 (38, 40) sts.

Row 2 and all wrong side rows: Purl.

Rows 3, 5, 7, 9, 11, 13, and 15: Rep Row 1. At end of last row: 22 (24, 26) sts.

Row 17: Bind off 1 (2, 2) sts; knit across: 21 (22, 24) sts.

Row 19: Bind off 1 (1, 2) sts; knit across: 20 (21, 22) sts.

Rows 21, 23, 25, 27, and 29: Bind off 1 (1, 1) st. At end of Row 29: 15 (16, 17) sts.

Work in stockinette stitch until right front measures same as back.

Bind off.

Sew shoulder seams.

CENTER FRONT AND NECKLINE BAND

Row 1 (right side)**:** Hold piece with right side facing you; starting at lower right center front edge with smaller size needle and chenille yarn, pick up and knit 62 (64, 66) sts to shoulder seam, 22 sts along back neckline to shoulder seam, and 62 (64, 66) sts along left front to first row: 146 (150, 154) sts.

96

Rows 2 through 5: Knit.

Bind off.

SLEEVES

Row 1 (right side)**:** Hold piece with right side facing you and one side edge at top; with larger size needles and worsted weight, pick up and knit 48 (50, 50) sts between markers.

Row 2: Purl.

Work in stockinette stitch until sleeve measures 6 1/2" (7", 7"), ending by working a wrong side row.

With smaller size needle and chenille yarn, knit 5 rows.

Bind off.

Repeat for other sleeve.

Sew sleeve and side seams leaving markers in place.

TIES (make 4)

With crochet hook and worsted weight yarn, ch 60. Cut yarn, leaving ends for sewing.

On right front, sew one tie on inside side seam under sleeve at marked row and one tie on same row at center front.

Sew one tie on outside left front under sleeve at marked row and one tie on same row at center front. Remove markers. Tie knots in free end of each tie.

BERIBBONED AFGHAN

Size:
38" x 58"

MATERIALS
Worsted weight yarn,
  18 oz white
Note: *Photographed model was made
  in TLC® Amoré™ Color #3001 White*
29" size 10 (6 mm) circular needle
  (or size required for gauge)
Size G (4 mm) crochet hook
6 ½ yds 4 mm silk ribbon
6 ½ yds ¹⁄₁₆" satin ribbon
6 ½ yds ⅛" satin ribbon
6 ½ yds ⅛" organza ribbon

GAUGE
4 sts = 1" in garter stitch (knit
  every row)

FAN SHELL PATTERN STITCH
Special Abbreviation used in Patt St:
SSK (slip, slip, knit) = sl next 2 sts as
to knit (one at a time) to right-hand
needle; insert tip of left-hand needle
through these 2 slipped sts on right-
hand needle, then knit both sts tog.

Instructions
Cast on 114 sts loosely. Do not join;
work back and forth in rows. Knit
3 rows.

Now work in Fan Shell Patt St as
follows:

Row 1 (right side)**:** K1, K2 tog; YO, K2;
(YO, K1) 5 times; * YO, K4, (YO, K1) 5
times; rep from * to last 5 sts, YO, K2;
YO, K2 tog, K1.

Note: *Throughout patt, each YO
counts as one st.*

Row 2: K3, P2, K11; * P4, K11; rep
from * to last 5 sts, P2, K3.

Row 3: K5, P11; * K4, P11; rep from
* to last 5 sts, K5.

Row 4: K3, * P2 tog, P11, P2 tog
through back lps (abbreviated tbl); rep
from * to last 3 sts, K3.

Row 5: K1, K2 tog, YO; * SSK, K9, K2
tog; rep from * to last 3 sts, YO, K2
tog, K1.

Row 6: K3, * P2 tog, P7, P2 tog tbl;
rep from * to last 3 sts, K3.

Row 7: K5, (YO, K1) 5 times; * YO, K4, (YO, K1) 5 times; rep from * to last 5 sts, YO, K5.

Row 8: Rep Row 2.

Row 9: K1, K2 tog; YO, K2, P11; * K4, P11; rep from * to last 5 sts, K2, YO, K2 tog, K1.

Row 10: Rep Row 4.

Row 11: K3, * SSK, K9, K2 tog; rep from * to last 3 sts, K3.

Row 12: Rep Row 6.

Rep Rows 1 through 12, 16 times more. Then rep Row 1 once more.

Next Row (wrong side)**:** K3, K2 tog, K11; * (K2 tog) twice, K11; rep from * to last 5 sts, K2 tog, K3.

Next Row: K3, K2 tog, K9; * (K2 tog) twice, K9; rep from * to last 5 sts, K2 tog, K3.

Next Row: K3, K2 tog, K7; * (K2 tog) twice, K7; rep from * to last 5 sts, K2 tog, K3. Bind off loosely in knit.

Weave in all ends.

RIBBON FRINGE

Follow basic fringe instructions on page 124. Cut both ribbon and yarn strands 14" long. Use two strands of yarn together with 3 different types of ribbon for each knot. Using five strands together, pull through from back with crochet hook, following photo for placement of ribbon fringe.

LITTLE GUY'S NORWEGIAN SWEATER

Size: 12 - 18 months

Finished Garment
Chest Measurement: 26"

MATERIALS

Sportweight yarn,
   5 ozs blue
   3 ozs white
Note: *Photographed model was
   made with Lion Brand Wool-Ease®
   Sportweight, Colors #196 Blueberry
   Twist and #099 Fisherman)*
14" Size 5 (3.75 mm) straight knitting
   needles
14" Size 6 (4 mm) straight knitting
   needles (or size required for gauge)
One medium stitch holder
Two small stitch holders
Size 16 tapestry needle
Four yarn bobbins
Four 3/4" diameter buttons
Sewing needle
Matching sewing thread

GAUGE

27 sts = 4" with larger size needles in
   stockinette st (knit one row, purl
   one row)

Notes

1. To make it easier to work with two
colors at the same time, wind the yarn
around bobbins and work with the bobbins rather than with two balls of yarn
once chart work has begun.

2. In working from the charts, read knit
rows from right to left; read purl rows
left to right.

3. When working with two colors, carry
unused yarn loosely across the back of
the work.

Instructions

BACK

With smaller needles and blue cast on
88 sts.

RIBBING

Row 1 (wrong side)**:** * K1, P1; rep from
* across.

Rows 2 through 7: Rep Row 1.

Change to larger size needles.

BODY

Row 1: (right side) Knit.

Row 2: Purl

Remainder of front pattern is worked in
stockinette st in two colors, following
Body Chart. Be sure yarn is wound on
bobbins; carry unused yarn loosely across
back of work. When changing colors,
always bring new color up from under
old color to prevent holes in work.

When the chart has been completed
work stock st in blue until piece measures 11 1/2" from cast on edge.

NECK

With smaller size needles work K1, P1
ribbing for 1", ending by working a
wrong side row.

Next Row: Work K1, P1 ribbing on first
29 st for right shoulder; bind off next
30 sts in ribbing for center back; join a
second ball of yarn and work 29 sts in
K1, P1 ribbing for left shoulder.

With separate yarn, work rem 29 sts on
each shoulder for 1/2" in K1, P1 ribbing.
Bind off in ribbing.

FRONT

Work same as back until piece measures
10 1/2", ending by working a purl row.

Body Chart

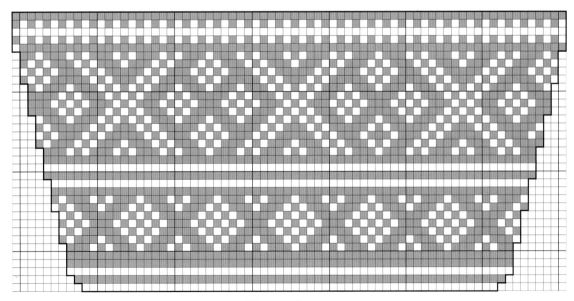

Sleeve Chart

continued on page 102

LITTLE GUY'S NORWEGIAN SWEATER
continued

NECK

Continuing to follow chart, K33 for left shoulder; place next 22 sts on medium stitch holder for front neck; join second bobbins of blue and white yarn, K33 for right shoulder. Work both shoulders at the same time.

Row 1: P31. Put 2 stitches on small stitch holder. With second bobbins, P33.

Row 2: K31. Put 2 sts on small st holder. With other bobbins, K31.

Row 3: P30. Put one st on small holder (3 sts now on holder), With other bobbins, P31.

Row 4: K30. Put one st on small holder(3 sts now on holder). With other bobbins, K30.

Row 5: P29. Put one st on small stitch holder (4 sts on holder) With other bobbins, P30.

Row 6: K29. Put one st on st holder (4 sts on holder) , With other bobbins, K29.

Row 7: P29. With second bobbins, P29.

Row 8: K29, K 4 sts from small stitch holder. Pick up and knit 22 sts on large stitch holder,knit 4 sts from small stitch holder, K29: 88 sts.

With one set of bobbins, work in patt until piece measures 11 ½" from cast-on edge to shoulders.

RIBBING

With smaller needles and blue.

Rows 1 through 6: * K1, P1, rep from * across

Row 7 (buttonhole row)**:** Working ribbing as established (rib 8 sts, bind off 3 sts for buttonhole) twice; rib to last 22 sts, (bind off 3 sts, rib 8 sts) twice.

Rep Row 1, if necessary, until the piece measures 13" from the cast on edge. Work ribbing as established; cast on 3 sts over those bound-off for each buttonhole.

Bind off in ribbing.

SLEEVES (make 2)

With blue, cast on 48 sts on smaller needles.

Rows 1 through 7: *K1, P1; rep from * across row.

With larger needles, work two rows of stock st, increasing one st at beg and end of each row: 52 sts.

Then follow Sleeve Chart, working in stock st, and continuing to increase one st at beg and end of next 3 rows: 58 sts. Then increase 1 st at beg and end of every 4 rows, 8 times: 74 sts.

When the chart has been completed work stock st rows of blue until piece measures 8" from cast on edge.

Bind off loosely.

FINISHING

Step 1: Lay front and back pieces flat with right sides facing and top ribbings together. Pin bind-off rows together at one side edge. Place one sleeve on top of front and back pieces with right sides together. Matching side edges of sleeve with rows on body, pin to hold. Sew sleeve to body, leaving shoulder open. Repeat for other sleeve.

Step 2: Sew sleeve and side seams.

Step 3: With sewing needle and matching thread, sew buttons opposite buttonholes.

THE LITTLE BLACK DRESS

Designed by Kim Britt

Size:
Chest measures 20"

MATERIALS

Worsted weight chenille yarn,
   10 oz black

Note: *Photographed model was made in Lion Brand Chenille Sensations Color # 153 Black*

14" Size 8 (5 mm) straight knitting needles (or size required for gauge)

16" Size 8 (5 mm) circular knitting needle

Large stitch holder

3 pearl buttons with shank, 3/8" diameter

Sewing thread and needle

Tapestry needle

GAUGE

4 sts and 5 rows = 1"
   in knit one, purl one ribbing

Instructions

YOKE

Note: *Yoke front and back are worked in one piece.*

BACK

Starting at back with straight needles, cast on 48 sts.

Ribbing Row: * K1, P1; rep from * across row.

Rep Ribbing Row until piece measures 3". Yoke is now divided and right and left sides are worked with separate skeins of yarn.

Divided Rows

Row 1 (right side)**:** Knit next 24 sts for right back; drop first skein; with second skein K24 for left back.

Row 2: P20, K4 for buttonhole band, with next skein, K4 for button band, P20.

Row 3: K24; with next skein, K1, loosely BO next 2 sts for buttonhole, K20.

Row 4: P20, K1, turn work to cast on 2 sts over the bound-off st, turn, K1; with next skein, K4, P20.

Row 5 through 10: Rep Rows 1 and 2, three times

Row 11 through 12: Rep Rows 3 and 4 once.

Row 13 through 18: Rep Rows 1 and 2 three times.

Rows 19 through 20: Rep Rows 3 and 4.

Row 21 through 22: Rep rows 1 and 2.

Mark last row to indicate top of back.

FRONT

While continuing to work each side of yoke with separate skeins, shape neck opening.

Row 1 (right side)**:** K24, drop yarn; with next skein, bind off 12 sts, K12.

Row 2: P12, drop yarn; with next skein, bind off 12 sts, P12.

Row 3: With separate skeins of yarn, knit across each side of yoke

Row 4: With separate skeins of yarn, purl across each side of yoke

Row 5: K11, inc in next st; with next skein, inc in first st, K11: 13 sts each side of yoke.

Row 6: Rep Row 4.

Row 7 and 8: Rep rows 3 and 4.

Row 9: Rep Row 5: 14 sts each side.

Row 10 through 13: Rep Rows 6 through 9: 15 sts each side.

Row 14 through 16: Rep rows 6 through 8.

Row 17: K15, loosely cast on 12 sts; with same skein knit 15 sts on other side of yoke: 42 sts. Cut second skein, from now on work with one skein only.

Row 5: * K in front and in back lp of next st: inc made; rep from * in each st: 168 sts.

Row 6: Knit.

Rep Row 6 until piece measures 15" from start of skirt.

Bottom Border

Row 1: Purl.

Row 2: Knit.

Row 3: Purl.

Bind off loosely as to knit.

NECK EDGING

Hold work with right side facing; with circular needle pick up and knit 58 sts evenly around neck edge; do not join.

Row 18: Purl.

Row 19: Knit.

Row 20: Purl

Rep Rows 19 and 20 until piece measures 11" from cast-on edge.

Ribbing Row: * K1, P1; rep from * across.

Rep Ribbing Row for 3", ending by working a wrong-side row. Place all sts on stitch holder.

SLEEVES

Hold work with right side facing; with straight needles pick up and knit 52 sts along one side of yoke from cast-on edge to sts on holder.

Row 1: Knit.

Row 2: K1, P50 sts, K1.

Rep Rows 1 and 2 until sleeve measures 4 1/2", ending by working a right side row.

Knit three more rows, bind off.

Work second sleeve in same manner on opposite edge of yoke.

SKIRT

With right side facing, and back yoke bottom edge on top, join yarn at upper right-hand corner; with circular needle pick up and knit 42 sts along cast-on edge; K42 sts from holder: 84 sts; join, mark to indicate beg of rnd. Sl marker on each rnd.

Rows 1 through 4: Knit.

Row 1: Knit.

Row 2: Knit

Bind off as to knit.

FINISHING

Weave in all ends. Sew sleeve seams.

OLD-FASHIONED BABY LAYETTE

Size: Newborn to 3 mos.

Finished Garment   approx.
Chest Measurement: 19½"

MATERIALS

Worsted weight yarn,
  8 oz cream
  2 oz green
Note: *Photographed model was made with TLC® Amoré™, Colors #3102 Vanilla and #3625 Celery*
14" Size 6 (4 mm) straight knitting needles (or size required for gauge)
24" Size 6 (4 mm) circular knitting needle
Three ½" shank buttons
3 yds ½" wide cream ribbon
Two bobbins

GAUGE

4 sts = 1" in stockinette st
  (knit one row, purl one row)

Note: YRN – *This abbeviation stands for Yarn Round Needle, which is how a YO is worked after a knit st and before a purl st. Take yarn from back to front under needle, then wrap to back over needle, and bring to front again under needle, which brings it completely around the needle and into the purl position.*

Sweater Instructions

BACK

Bottom Border

With green, cast on 72 sts.

Rows 1 through 6: Knit. Finish off green.

BODY

Rows 1 through 3: With cream, knit.

Row 4: K2, purl to last 2 sts, K2.

Row 5: K2, * YRN, P1, P3 tog; P1, YO, K2; rep from * across.

Row 6: K2, purl to last 2 sts, K2.

Row 7: Knit.

Rep Rows 4 through 7 for pattern.

Work even in patt until piece measures 5¾", ending by working Row 6.

Decrease Row (right side): K2; * K2 tog; rep from * to last 2 sts. K2: 38 sts

Next Row: K1, P36, K1.

Attach green, do not cut cream; knit 2 rows green, cut green. Pick up cream.

SHAPE ARMHOLE

Row 1 (right side): K1, K2 tog, K to last 3 sts, K2 tog. K1: 36 sts.

Row 2: K1, purl to last st, K1.

Rows 3 through 8: Rep Rows 1 and 2; at end of Row 8: 30 sts.

Row 9: Knit.

Row 10: K1, purl to last st, K1.

Rep Rows 9 and 10 until armhole measures 3¼", ending by working a purl row.

Continuing to work in stock st, bind off 4 sts at beg of next 4 rows. Bind off rem 14 sts.

RIGHT FRONT

Note: *Wind green on bobbin for Fronts.*

Bottom Border

With green bobbin, cast on 35 sts and knit six rows.

BODY

Row 1 (right side):With green, K4. Join cream and knit across.

Row 2: With cream K1, purl to last 4 sts; with green, K4.

Row 3: With green, K4. With cream knit across.

Row 4: With cream, K1, purl to last 4 sts; with green, K4.

Row 5: With green, K4; with cream, K2, * YRN, P1, P3 tog, P1, YO, K2; rep from * to last st, K1.

Row 6: With cream, K1. purl to last 4 sts; with green, K4.

Row 7: With green, K4; with cream, knit across.

Rep rows 4 through 7 for patt.

Work even in patt until piece measures 5¾", ending by working Row 6 of patt.

Decrease Row (right side): With green,

K4; with cream, K2, * K2 tog. Rep to last st, K1: 21 sts.

Next Row: With cream, P17. With green, K4. Drop cream, do not cut.

BUTTONHOLE AND GARTER ST BAND

Row 1: With green, K1, bind off 2 sts, knit across row.

Row 2: K18, cast on 2 sts, K1.

SHAPE ARMHOLE

Row 1: With green, K4; with cream, K14, K2 tog, K1: 20sts.

Row 2: With cream, K1, P15; with green, K4.

Row 3: With green, K4; with cream, K13, K2 tog, K1: 19 sts.

Row 4: With cream, K1, P14; with green, K4.

Row 5: With green, K4; with cream, K12, K2 tog, K1: 18 sts.

Row 6: With cream, K1, P13; with green, K4.

Row 7 (buttonhole row): With green, K1, bind off 2 sts, K1, with cream, K11, K2 tog, K1: 15 sts.

Row 8: With cream, K1, P 12; with green, K1, cast on 2 sts, K1: 17 sts.

Row 9: With green, K4; with cream, K13.

Row 10: With cream, K1, P12; with green, K4.

Rows 11 through 14: Rep Rows 9 and 10, twice.

Row 15 (buttonhole row): With green, K1, bind off 2 sts, K1; with cream, K13: 15 sts.

Row 16: With cream, K1, P12; with green, K1, cast on 2 sts, K1: 17 sts.

Rep Rows 9 and 10 until armhole measures 2¼", ending by working a knit row.

SHAPE SHOULDER

Row 1: With cream, bind off first 6 sts as to purl, P7; with green, K4: 11 sts.

Row 2: With green, K4, with cream, K4, K2 tog, K1: 10 sts.

Row 3: With cream, K1, P2 tog, P3; with green, K4: 9 sts.

Row 4: With green, K4, with cream, K2, K2 tog, K1: 8 sts

Row 5: With cream, K1, P3; with green, K4.

Row 6: With green, K4; with cream, K4.

Rep Rows 5 and 6 until armhole measures 3¼", ending at armhole edge.

SHAPE NECK

Row 1 (wrong side): With cream, K2 tog, P2 tog; with green, K4: 6 sts.

Row 2: With green, K4; with cream, K2.

Row 3: With cream, bind off 1 st; with green, bind off one st; K3: 4 sts.

Row 4: With green, K4. With green, bind off rem 4 sts.

LEFT FRONT

Bottom Border

With bobbin, cast on 35 sts and knit 6 rows.

Cut green yarn.

continued on page 108

OLD-FASHIONED BABY LAYETTE

continued

Row 1: With cream, knit to last 4 sts; attach green bobbin, K4 with green.

Row 2: With green, K4; with cream, purl to last st, K1.

Row 3: With cream, knit to last 4 sts, with green, K4.

Row 4: With green, K4; with cream, purl to last st K1.

Row 5: With cream, K3, * YRN, P1, P3 tog, P1, YO, K2; rep from * to last 4 sts, K4 with green.

Row 6: With green, K4; with cream, purl to last st, K1.

Row 7: With cream, knit to last 4 sts; with green, K4.

Rep Rows 4 through 7 for pattern.

Work even in pattern until piece measures 5¾", ending by working Row 6 of patt.

Decrease Row (right side)**:** With cream, K1, (K2 tog) 14 times, K2; with green, K4: 21 sts.

Next Row: With green, K4, cut green; with cream, P16, K1. Do not cut cream.

Join green and knit two rows for garter st band. Cut green.

SHAPE ARMHOLE

Row 1: With cream, K1, K2 tog, K14; join green bobbin, K4: 20 sts.

Row 2: With green, K4; with cream, P15. K1

Row 3: With cream, K1, K2 tog, K13; with green, K4: 19 sts

Row 4: With green, K4; with cream, P14, K1.

Row 5: With cream, K1, K2tog, K12; with green, K4: 18sts.

Row 6: With green, K4; with cream, P13, K1

Row 7: With cream , K1, K2 tog, K11; with green, K4: 17sts.

Row 8: With green, K4; with cream, P12, K1.

Row 9: With cream, K13, with green K4.

Row 10: With green, K4. With cream, P12, K1.

Rep Rows 9 and 10 until armhole measures 2¼" or is same length as buttonhole edge on right front, ending by working a purl row.

SHAPE SHOULDER

Row 1: With cream, bind off 6 sts as to knit, K6; with green, K4: 11 sts.

Row 2: With green, K4; with cream P4, P2 tog, K1: 10 sts.

Row 3: With cream, K1, K2tog, K3; with green, K4: 9 sts.

Row 4: With green, K4; with cream, P2, P2 tog, K1: 8 sts.

Row 5: With cream, K4; with green, K4.

Row 6: With green, K4; with cream, P3, K1.

Row 7: With cream, K4; with green, K4.

Work even on 8 sts until piece measures same as back ending at armhole edge.

SHAPE NECK

Row 1 (right side)**:** With cream, (K2 tog) twice; with green, K4: 6 sts.

Row 2: With green, K4; with cream, P1, K1.

Row 3: With cream, bind off 1 st; with green, bind off 1 st, K3: 4 sts.

Row 4: With green, K4.

Bind off 4 sts.

SLEEVE (make 2)

With green, cast on 21 sts.

Knit six rows with green for garter st border. Cut green. Attach cream.

Row 1 (right side)**:** Knit.

Rows 2 and 3: Knit.

Row 4: K1, purl to last st, K1.

Row 5: K1, * YRN, P1, P3 tog; P1, YO, K2; rep from * across, ending last rep with K1.

Row 6: K1, purl to last st, K1.

Row 7: Knit.

Rep Rows 4 through 7 for patt until piece measures 6 1/2"

SHAPE CAP

Keeping patt as established, bind off one st at beg of next two rows and then dec one st at each end of every other row until 9 sts remain on needle. Bind off all sts.

FINISHING

Sew shoulder seams. Sew side and sleeve seams. Sew sleeves into armholes.

COLLAR

Hold garment with wrong side facing you and neck at top.

Row 1: Join green in second st of left front band, pick up and knit 12 sts across left front neck edge to shoulder seam, 14 sts across back neck edge, and 12 sts across right front neck edge, ending in second st of front band: 38 sts.

Row 2: Knit.

Row 3: K4; * inc by knitting in front and in back of next st, K2; rep from * to last 4 sts, K4: 48 sts.

Row 4: K4, purl to last 4 sts, K4.

Row 5: Knit.

Rep Rows 4 and 5 until collar measures 1" from neck edge, ending by working a knit row.

Knit 4 more rows for garter st border, bind off.

Sew buttons on left front opposite buttonholes.

Bonnet Instructions

BORDER

Starting at front edge with green, cast on 52 sts.

Rows 1 through 4: Knit

Row 5: K13 * inc (knit in front and back of stitch) in next st, K5; rep from * 4 times more, K9: 57 sts. Finish off green.

CROWN

Row 1: With cream, K2, purl to last 2 sts, K2.

Row 2: * K2, YRN, P1, P3 tog; P1, YO; rep from * to last st, K1.

Row 3: K2, purl to last 2 sts, K2.

Row 4: Knit.

Rep Rows 1 through 4 until piece measures 5" from cast-on edge, ending by working Row 1 or Row 3.

BACK SHAPING

Row 1: K39, sl 1 as to knit, K1, PSSO; turn, leaving rem 16 sts unworked.

Row 2: Sl 1 as to purl, P20, sl 1 as to purl, P2 tog, PSSO; turn, leaving rem 16 sts unworked.

Row 3: Sl 1 as to purl, K20, sl 1 as to knit, K1, PSSO; turn, leaving rem 15 sts unworked.

Row 4: Sl 1 as to purl, P20, P2 tog; turn, leaving rem 15 sts unworked.

Row 5: Sl 1 as to purl, K20, sl 1 as to knit, K1, PSSO; turn, leaving rem 14 sts unworked.

Row 6: Sl 1 as to purl, P20, P2 tog; turn, leaving rem 14 sts unworked.

Row 7: Sl 1 as to purl, K20, sl 1 as to knit, K1, PSSO; turn, leaving rem 13 sts unworked.

Row 8: Sl 1 as to purl, P20, P2 tog; turn, leaving rem 13 sts unworked.

Row 9: Sl 1 as to purl, K20, sl 1 as to knit, K1, PSSO; turn, leaving rem 12 sts unworked.

Row 10: Sl 1 as to purl, P20, P2 tog; turn, leaving rem 12 sts unworked.

Row 11: Sl 1 as to purl, K20, sl 1 as to knit, K1, PSSO; turn, leaving rem 11 sts unworked.

Row 12: Sl 1 as to purl, P20, P2 tog; turn, leaving rem 11 sts unworked.

Row 13: Sl 1 as to purl, K20, sl 1 as to knit, K1, PSSO; turn, leaving rem 10 sts unworked.

Row 14: Sl 1 as to purl, P20, P2 tog; turn, leaving rem 10 sts unworked.

Row 15: Sl 1 as to purl, K20, sl 1 as to knit, K1, PSSO; turn, leaving rem 9 sts unworked.

Row 16: Sl 1 as to purl, P20, P2 tog; turn, leaving rem 9 sts unworked.

Row 17: Sl 1 as to purl, K20, sl 1 as to knit, K1, PSSO; turn, leaving rem 8 sts unworked.

Row 18: Sl 1 as to purl, P20, P2 tog; turn, leaving rem 8 sts unworked.

Row 19: Sl 1 as to purl, K20, sl 1 as to knit, K1, PSSO; turn, leaving rem 7 sts unworked.

continued on page 110

OLD-FASHIONED BABY LAYETTE

continued

Row 20: Sl 1 as to purl, P20, P2 tog; turn, leaving rem 7 sts unworked.

Row 21: Sl 1 as to purl, K20, sl 1 as to knit, K1, PSSO; turn, leaving rem 6 sts unworked.

Row 22: Sl 1 as to purl, P20, P2 tog; turn, leaving rem 6 sts unworked.

Row 23: Sl 1 as to purl, K20, sl 1 as to knit, K1, PSSO; turn, leaving rem 5 sts unworked.

Row 24: Sl 1 as to purl, P20, P2 tog; turn, leaving rem 5 sts unworked.

Row 25: Sl 1 as to purl, K20, sl 1 as to knit, K1, PSSO; turn, leaving rem 4 sts unworked.

Row 26: Sl 1 as to purl, P20, P2 tog; turn, leaving rem 4 sts unworked.

Row 27: Sl 1 as to purl, K20, sl 1 as to knit, K1, PSSO; turn, leaving rem 3 sts unworked.

Row 28: Sl 1 as to purl, P20, P2 tog; turn, leaving rem 3 sts unworked.

Row 29: Sl 1 as to purl, K20, sl 1 as to knit, K1, PSSO; turn, leaving rem 2 sts unworked.

Row 30: Sl 1 as to purl, P20, P2 tog; turn, leaving rem 2 sts unworked.

Row 31: Sl 1 as to purl, K20, sl 1 as to knit, K2 tog, PSSO.

Row 32: Sl 1 as to purl, P20, P3 tog: 22 sts.

Cut cream.

NECKBAND

Hold bonnet with right side facing you and neck edge at top; join green yarn at front edge at upper right-hand corner.

Knit across neck edge as follows: pick up and knit 16 sts evenly spaced along side of bonnet to left hand needle; K1 working across back of bonnet, * sl 1 as if to knit, K2 tog, PSSO; rep from * 6 times more. Pick up and knit 16 sts evenly spaced along rem side edge to front edge: 40 sts.

Knit 5 rows for border. Bind off.

FINISHING

Attach one piece of ribbon approx 22" to each side of front edge, making a small bow (see photo).

BOOTIES INSTRUCTIONS (make 2)

Note: *To increase (inc), knit in front and in back of specified st.*

Starting at bottom edge, with cream, cast on 28 sts.

Sole
Row 1 (right side)**:** K1, inc in next st; K10, inc in each of next 4 sts; K10, inc in next st, K1: 34 sts.

Row 2: Knit.

Row 3: K1, inc in next st; K13; inc in each of next 4 sts; K13, inc in next st, K1: 40 sts.

Row 4: Knit.

Row 5: K1, inc in next st; K16; inc in each of next 4 sts; K16, inc in next st. K1: 46 sts.

Rep Row 4 until piece measures 1 1/2" from cast-on edge, ending by working a right-side row.

Instep
Row 1 (wrong side)**:** K17, K2 tog; K8, K2 tog; turn, leaving rem 17 sts unworked.

Row 2 (right side)**:** Sl 1 as to purl, K2, YRN, P1, P3 tog, P1, YO, K1, K2 tog; turn, leaving rem 16 sts unworked.

Row 3: Sl 1 as to purl, P8, K2 tog; turn, leaving rem 16 sts unworked.

Row 4: Sl 1 as to purl, K8, K2 tog; turn, leaving rem 15 sts unworked.

Row 5: Sl 1 as to purl, P8, K2 tog; turn, leaving rem 15 sts unworked.

Row 6: Sl 1 as to purl, K2, YRN, P1, P3 tog, P1, YO, K1, K2 tog; turn, leaving rem 14 sts unworked.

Row 7: Sl 1 as to purl, P8, K2 tog; turn, leaving rem 14 sts unworked.

Row 8: Sl 1 as to purl, K8, K2 tog; turn, leaving rem 13 sts unworked.

Row 9: Sl 1 as to purl, P8, K2 tog; turn, leaving rem 13 sts unworked.

Row 10: Sl 1 as to purl, K2, YRN, P1, P3 tog, P1, YO, K1, K2 tog; turn, leaving rem 12 sts unworked.

Row 11: Sl 1 as to purl, P8, K2 tog; turn, leaving rem 12 sts unworked.

Row 12: Sl 1 as to purl, K8, K2 tog; turn, leaving rem 11 sts unworked.

Row 13: Sl 1 as to purl, P8, K2 tog; turn, leaving rem 11 sts unworked.

Row 14: Sl 1 as to purl, K2, YRN, P1, P3 tog, P1, YO, K1, K2 tog; turn, leaving rem 10 sts unworked.

Row 15: Sl 1 as to purl, P8, K2 tog; turn, leaving rem 10 sts unworked.

Row 16: Sl 1 as to purl, K8, K2 tog; turn, leaving rem 9 sts unworked.

Row 17: Sl 1 as to purl, P8, K2 tog. Do not turn; knit rem 9 sts.

Row 18: K12, YRN, P1, P3 tog, P1, YO, K1, K2 tog, K8: 27 sts.

Row 19: K9, P8, K10.

Ankle

Row 1 (eyelet row)**:** K1, (YO, K2 tog) 6 times; YO, K1, (YO, K2 tog) 6 times; YO, K1: 29 sts.

Row 2: Knit.

Row 3: K4 * K2, YRN, P1, P3 tog, P1, YO. Rep from * to last 4 sts, K4.

Row 4: K2, P to last 2 sts, K2.

Row 5: Knit.

Row 6: Rep Row 4.

Rep rows 3 to 6, 2 times more. Then work Rows 3 and 4 once more.

Cut cream. Attach green and knit 5 rows. Bind off.

With matching colors, sew back and sole seam. Cut two 20" lengths of ribbon and weave through eyelet row of each bootie. Tie in a bow and trim ends.

AFGHAN

Size:
38" x 38"

MATERIALS
Worsted weight yarn,
   18 oz cream
   6 oz green
Note: *Photographed model was made with TLC® Amoré™ Colors #3103 Vanilla and # 3625 Celery*
29" Size 6 (4 mm) circular knitting
   needle (or size required for gauge)
Two yarn bobbins

GAUGE
4 sts = 1" in stockinette st
   (knit one row, purl one row)

NOTES
1. Wind two bobbins with green to use at start and end of each row. When changing colors be sure to bring the new color up from under the old color to prevent holes.

2. YRN. This abbreviation means yarn round needle and is used when working a YO after a knit stitch and before a purl stitch. Wrap yarn completely around needle before working next stitch.

Instructions
Cast on 147 sts with green. Do not join; work back and forth in rows.

Knit 6 rows.

Now begin pattern, using bobbins for green edge stitches and skein for cream center.

Row 1: With green K4; join cream, purl to last 4 sts, K4 green.

Row 2: With green, K4; with cream, K1 * YRN, P1, P3 tog; P1, YO, K2; rep from * to last 9 sts; YRN, P1, P3 tog, YO, K1; K4 green.

Row 3: With green, K4; with cream, purl to last 4 sts; K4 green.

Row 4: With green, K4; with cream, knit to last 4 sts, K4 green.

Rep rows 1 through 4 until afghan measures about 37", ending by working Row 1.

Finish off cream; with green, knit 6 rows. Bind off all stitches.

ANGEL TOP

Size: Newborn to 3 mos.

Finished Garment approx.
Chest Measurement: 19"

MATERIALS

Worsted weight yarn,
  6 ozs cream
  1 oz green
Note: *Photographed model was
made with TLC® Amoré Colors
#3103 Vanilla and #3625 Celery*
24" Size 6 (4 mm) circular knitting
  needle, (or size required for gauge)
14" Size 6 (4 mm) straight knitting
  needles
Stitch markers
Tapestry needle
Three 1/2" shank buttons

GAUGE

4 sts = 1" in stockinette st
  (knit one row, purl one row)

Bodice Instructions

With green, starting at neck edge with
circular needle, cast on 41 sts. Do not
join; work back and forth in rows.

Row 1 (wrong side)**:** Knit.

Row 2 and 3: Knit.

Row 4 (buttonhole row)**:** K2, YO (for
buttonhole), K2 tog; knit rem sts.

Row 5: K4 * P1, YRN, P1, K1; rep from
to last 4 sts; K4: 52 sts. Cut green.

Row 6: Attach cream. K4; * P1, sl 1 as
to knit, K2, PSSO; rep from * to last 4
sts, K4: 41 sts.

Row 7: K4 *P1, YRN, P1, K1; rep from
* to last 4 sts; K4: 52 sts.

Rows 8 through 12: Knit.

Row 13: K2, * P1, YRN, P1, K1; rep
from * to last 2 sts, K2: 68 sts.

Row 14: K2, * P1, sl 1 as to knit, K2,
PSSO; rep from * to last 2 sts, K2:
52 sts.

Row 15: Rep Row 13: 68 sts.

Row 16 (buttonhole row)**:** K2, YO (for
buttonhole) K2 tog; knit rem sts.

Rows 17 through 19: Knit.

Row 20: K3, inc (knit in front and back
of next st), knit to last 4 sts, inc, K3:
70 sts.

Row 21: K2, * P1, YRN, P1, K1; rep
from * to last 2 sts. K2: 92 sts.

Row 22: K2, * P1, sl 1 as if to knit, K2,
PSSO; rep from * to last 2 sts, K2: 70 sts.

Row 23: Rep row 21: 92 sts.

Rows 24 through 27: Knit.

Row 28 (buttonhole and dividing row)**:**
K2, YO (for buttonhole), K2 tog; (YO,
K1) 8 times; YO, K2, inc; place marker
on needle; inc; K2, (YO, K1) 10 times,
YO, K2, inc; place marker on needle; inc;
K2, (YO, K1) 24 times; YO, K2, inc;
place marker on needle; inc; K2, (YO,
K1) 10 times; YO, K2, inc; place marker
on needle; inc; K2, (YO, K1) 8 times; YO,
K4. (You now have 165 sts on needle;
25 across each back section; 29 sts
across each sleeve, and 57 sts across
the front.) **Note:** *On following rows,
slip markers as you come to them.*

Row 29: K4; purl to last 4 sts; K4.

Row 30: K24, inc; sl marker, inc; K27,
inc; sl marker, inc, K55, inc; sl marker,
inc; K27, inc; sl marker, inc, K24: 173 sts.

Rows 31, 33, 35 and 37: Rep row 29.

Row 32: K25, inc, sl marker, inc, K29,
inc; sl marker, inc, K57, inc; sl marker,
inc; K29, inc; sl marker; inc; K 25: 181 sts.

Row 34: K26, inc; sl marker, inc, K31,
inc; sl marker, inc, K59, inc; sl marker,
inc; K 31, inc, sl marker, inc, K26: 189 sts.

Row 36: K27, inc; sl marker, inc; K33,
inc; sl marker, inc, K61, inc; sl marker,
inc; K33, inc; sl marker, inc, K27: 197 sts.

Row 38: K28, inc; sl marker, inc; K35 ,
inc; sl marker, inc, K63, inc; sl marker,
inc; K35, inc; sl marker, inc, K28: 205
sts. (30 sts across each back section;
39 sts across each sleeve and 67 sts
across front).

Row 39: K4, purl to last 4 sts, K4.

Row 40 (Dividing row)**:** K30, remove marker. Drop yarn but do not cut as it will be used later. Join new skein of cream yarn. Change to straight needles and continue with new skein of yarn as follows: cast on 1 st, inc in next st, knit across 37 sts of right sleeve, inc in last st. Drop marker and leave rem sts on circular needle to work later: 42 sts (for sleeve).

SLEEVE

Note: Work on 42 sts of right sleeve only with straight needles.

Row 1: K1, purl to last st, K1.

Row 2: K1 * YRN, P1, P3 tog, P1, YO, K2. Rep from * across to last 6 sts, YRN, P1, P3 tog, P1, YO, K1.

Row 3: K1, Purl to last st, K1.

Row 4: Knit

Rows 5 through 12: Rep rows 1 through 4 twice.

Row 13: Rep row 1

Row 14: Rep row 2.

Row 15: Rep row 3. At end of row, cut cream.

Row 16: Attach green. * K2 tog, rep from * to end of row: 21 sts.

With green, knit 4 rows for garter st border.

Bind off in knit. Sew underarm seam.

With circular needle and attached cream yarn, continue on Row 40 of bodice as follows:

Row 40 (continued)**:** With right side facing you, pick up and knit 2 sts from sleeve underarm, then K67 sts across front. Drop yarn but do not cut as it will be used later. Join new skein of cream yarn. Change to straight needles and continue with new skein of yarn. Cast on 1 st, inc in next st, knit across 37 sts of right sleeve, inc in last st.

Drop marker and leave rem sts on circular needle to work later: 42 sleeve sts.

Work Left Sleeve same as for Right Sleeve.

When left sleeve is complete, return to sts on circular needle.

back

Row 40 (continued)**:** With right side facing you, pick up and knit 2 sts from sleeve underarm, working across back, knit 30 sts. Total sts on needle: 131 sts (30 sts left back, 2 sts underarm, 67 sts front, 2 sts underarm, 30 right back).

Row 41 (wrong side)**:** (K2 tog) 2 times; purl to last 4 sts, (K2 tog) 2 times: 127 sts.

Row 42: K1 * YRN, P1, P3 tog, P1, YO, K2, rep from * across to last 7 sts, YRN, P1, P3 tog, P1, YO, K2 tog: 126 sts.

Note: Back opening is now completed. DO NOT TURN. Place a marker on needle to indicate beg and end of each rnd. Move marker at the beg of each rnd. Join and work in rounds.

Rnd 1: Knit.

Rnd 2: Knit.

Rnd 3: Knit.

Rnd 4: K1 * YRN, P1, P3 tog, P1, YO, K2; rep from * around to last 6 sts, YRN, P1, P3 tog, P1, YO, K1.

Rep rounds 1 through 4 until piece measures 7" from armholes. Repeat Round 1. Cut cream and attach green. Knit 1 round, purl 1 round twice. Bind off loosely in knit.

Weave in all ends. Sew on buttons

CRAYON STRIPES

back

Size: 3 years

Finished Garment Chest Measurement:	30"

MATERIALS

Sport weight yarn,
- 3 ½ oz bright green
- 3 ½ oz dark green
- 3 ½ oz navy
- 3 ½ oz yellow
- 5 ½ oz blue

Note: *Photographed model was made with Patons® Astra, Colors #2911 Spring Green, #2217 Country Green, #2849 Navy, #2941 School Bus Yellow and #2774 Medium Blue*

Size 6 (4 mm) straight knitting needles (or size required for gauge)

Size 4 (3.5 mm) knitting needles
16" Size 6 (4 mm) circular knitting needles
8" Size 6 (4 mm) double-pointed knitting needles
Four flat ½" yellow buttons (for sweater only)
Two small stitch holders (for sweater only)
One medium stitch holder (for sweater only)
Tapestry needle

GAUGE

6 sts and 8 rows = 1" with larger needles, in stockinette st (knit one row, purl one row).

Sweater Instructions

BACK

With smaller needles and yellow, cast on 80 sts.

Rows 1 through 8: * K1, P1, rep from * across.

Change to larger needles and bright green and work in stock st, starting with a knit row, in following color sequence:

12 rows bright green
12 rows blue
12 rows navy
12 rows yellow
12 rows bright green
12 rows blue
12 rows navy
4 rows yellow

Change to smaller needles and continuing with yellow, work in K1, P1 ribbing for 8 rows. Bind off.

FRONT

Note: *Front is worked in a solid color.*

With smaller needles and. blue, cast on 80 sts.

Rows 1 through 8: * K1, P1, rep from * across.

Change to larger needles and starting with a knit row, work in stock st until piece measures 9 ½" from end of ribbing, ending by working a purl row,

NECK AND SHOULDER SHAPING

Dividing Row: K30 for left shoulder. Place next 20 sts on medium stitch holder for front neck. Attach 2nd skein of yarn and K30 for right shoulder. Now work both shoulders at the same time with separate skeins of yarn.

Row 1: P28, put next 2 stitches on a small stitch holder. With 2nd skein, P30.

Row 2: K28, put next 2 sts on 2nd small stitch holder. With other skein, K28.

Row 3: P27, add next st to first small stitch holder (3 sts on holder). With other skein, P28.

Row 4: K27, add next st to 2nd small stitch holder (3 sts on holder). With other skein, K27.

Row 5: P26, add next st to 2nd small stitch holder (4 sts on holder). With other skein, K27.

Row 6: K26, add next st to 2nd small stitch holder (4 sts on holder). With other skein, K26.

Row 7: P26, with second skein, P26.

Row 8: With one skein only, K26, K4 sts from first small holder, K20 sts from medium stitch holder, K4 sts from second small stitch holder, K26 sts from needle: 80 sts. Finish off unused skein.

Continue working in stock st until piece measures same as back to start of K1, P1 ribbing. Change to smaller needles.

RIBBING

Row 1 through 6: * K1, P1;. rep from * across.

Row 7 (Buttonhole row)**:** (K1, P1) 4 times, bind off 3 sts. (P1, K1) 3 times, bind off 3 sts; * K1, P1; rep from * to last 20 sts; bind off 3 sts, (P1, K1) 3 times; bind off 3 sts, (K1, P1) 4 times.

Row 8: Work in ribbing as established, and cast on 3 sts over each 3-st bind off of previous row.

continued on page 116

CRAYON STRIPES
continued

Bind off all sts.

SLEEVE (make 2)

With smaller needles and yellow, cast on 42 sts.

Rows 1 through 4: * K1, P1, rep from * across. Finish off yellow.

Rows 5 through 8: With bright green, * K1, P1, rep from * across. Finish off bright green.

Change to larger needles and work in stock st in following color sequence:

4 rows navy
4 rows blue
4 rows navy
4 rows dk green
4 rows yellow
4 rows bright green

At the same time, work shaping as follows:

Row 9: Inc (knit in front and back of st) in first st, knit to last st, inc in last st: 44 sts.

Continuing in stock st and in color pattern, inc one st at beg and end of row every 5 rows, 10 times: 64 sts. Work even until piece measures 8" from cast-on row. Bind off.

ASSEMBLY

Sew buttons on back top ribbing opposite buttonholes on front. Lap Front over Back about ½" and tack at sleeve edge.

Sew sleeves at shoulder, centering sleeves, at shoulder center.

Sew sleeve and side seams, matching stripes.

Pants Instructions

Note: Pants are worked in two pieces.

LEFT HALF
Ribbing

Starting at waistline with smaller needles and yellow, cast on 66 sts.

Rows 1 through 4: * K1, P1; rep from * across. Finish off yellow.

Rows 5 and 6: With bright green, * K1, P1, rep from * across.

Row 7 (eyelet row)**:** * K1, P1, YO, P2 tog; rep from * to last 2 sts, K1, P1.

Row 8: * K1, P1, rep from * across. Finish off bright green.

Body

Change to larger needles and work in following color sequence throughout:

4 rows navy
4 rows blue
4 rows navy
4 rows dk green
4 rows yellow
4 rows bright green

Note: *On Row 1, shaping is done to add depth at the back of the pants. This is done by working a number of sts, then turning.*

Row 1: K8, turn, P8; K18, turn, P18; K28, turn, P28; K38, turn, P38.

Row 2 (right side)**:** Knit all 66 sts.

Work 6 rows in stock st.

Next Row: Inc in first st (to inc, work in front and back of st), work across: 67 sts.

Continue in stock st, working inc in first st of every eighth row 3 times: 70 sts. Work 11 more rows in stock st.

LEG

Row 1: K1, K2 tog, knit to last 3 sts; K2 tog, K1.

Row 2: Purl

Rep Rows 1 and 2 until 60 sts rem. Work even until leg measures 9" from beg of shaping. Change to smaller needles and work in K1, P1 ribbing for 10 rows.

CUFF

Change to larger needles.

Row 1: (K1, sl 1, K1, PSSO, K14, K2 tog, K1) three times: 54 sts.

Row 2: Knit.

Row 3: (K1, sl 1, K1, PSSO, K12, K2 tog, K1) three times: 48 sts.

Row 4: Knit.

Row 5: (K1, sl 1, K1, PSSO, K10, K2 tog, K1) three times: 42 sts.

Row 6: Knit.

Row 7: (K1, sl 1, K1, PSSO, K8, K2 tog, K1) three times: 36 sts.

Row 8: Knit.

Bind off.

RIGHT HALF

Work as for Left Side for ribbing and color stripe pattern.

Body

Row 1 (shaping row)**:** With larger needles, P8, turn, K8; P18, turn, K18; P28, turn, K28; P38, turn, K38.

Row 2: Purl all 66 sts.

Complete as for left half.

FINISHING

Hold right and left halves with right sides facing and sew together on each edge, being sure that longer back sections of each Row 1 are together.

continued on page 118

CRAYON STRIPES
continued

Carefully match rows.

Then sew both leg seams, matching rows.

Cord
Note: *Cord is worked from right side only; do not turn. Stitches will fold toward the wrong side to form a double thickness cord.*

With circular needle and. bright green, and leaving an 8″ end, cast on 3 sts.

Row 1: Knit. Slide sts to opposite end of needle; do not turn.

Row 2: Carry yarn across wrong side of sts; knit. Slid sts to opposite end of needle; do not turn.

Rep rows 1 and 2 until cord measures about 36″. Bind off, leaving an 8″ end for sewing. Thread yarn through tapestry needle and draw through inside of cord.

Thread cord through eyelet row and tie at front.

Hat Instructions
With yellow and circular needle, cast on. 110 sts. Join, being careful not to twist stitches. Place marker at start of round.

Work K1, P1 ribbing for 1½″, keeping color sequence as follows:

4 rows yellow
4 rows bright green
4 rows navy
4 rows blue
4 rows navy
4 rows dk green

Then work each rnd in stock st keeping color sequence until piece measures 6¼″ from cast-on edge. Then begin decreasing.

Note: *When sts can no longer be accommodated on circular needle, switch to double-pointed needles and continue working in rnds.*

Rnd 1: (K2, K2 tog) twice; K6; (K7, K2 tog) 10 times; (K2 tog) twice, K2: 96 sts.

Rnd 2: * K2, K2 tog; rep from * around: 72 sts.

Rnd 3: Knit.

Rnd 4: *K1, K2 tog; rep from * around: 48 sts.

Rnd 5: Knit.

Rnds 6 through 8: * K2 tog; rep from * around. At end of Rnd 8: 6 sts; finish off, leaving an 8″ yarn end.

Thread yarn into a tapestry needle and draw through rem sts; pull yarn tight and secure to inside.

Refresher Course
in Knitting

HOW TO KNIT

CASTING ON

There are many ways to cast on. If you are a beginner, try this easy method. Use only one needle. First, measure a length of yarn that will give you about 1" for each stitch to be cast on. First make a slip knot on the needle; make a yarn loop, leaving about 4" of yarn at the free end; inset the needle into the loop and draw up the yarn from the free end to make a loop on the needle.

Pull the yarn ends firmly, but not too tightly to form the slip knot on the needle. This slip knot counts as your first stitch.

Now begin the casting on:

Step One: Hold the needle with the slip knot in your right hand and with yarn from the skein to your left. With your left hand, make a yarn loop.

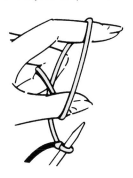

Insert the needle into the loop.

Step Two: Still holding the loop in your left hand, with your right hand, pick up the yarn from the skein and bring it back to front around the needle.

Step Three: Bring the needle through the loop and toward you; at the same time, pull gently on the yarn end to tighten the loop. Make it snug but not tight below the needle.

You have now cast on one stitch. Repeat Steps 1 through 3 for each additional stitch required.

THE KNIT STITCH

Step One: Hold the needle with the cast-on stitches in your left hand. Insert the point of the right needle into the first stitch, from right to left.

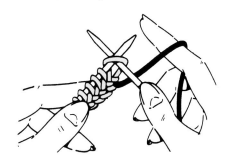

Step Two: With right index finger, bring the yarn under and over the point of the right needle.

Step Three: Draw the yarn through the stitch with the right needle point.

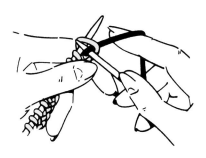

Step Four: Slip the loop on the left needle off, so the new stitch is entirely on the right needle.

You have now made one complete knit stitch.

THE PURL STITCH

The purl stitch is actually the reverse of the knit stitch. Instead of inserting the right needle point from left to right under the left needle (as you did for the knit stitch), you now insert it from right to left, in front of the left needle.

Step One: Insert the right needle from right to left, into the first stitch and in front of the left needle,

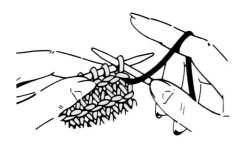

Step Two: Holding the yarn in front of the work (side toward you), bring it around the right needle counterclockwise.

Step Three: With right needle, pull the yarn back through the stitch.

Step Four: Slide the stitch off the left needle, leaving the new stitch on the right needle.

You have now made one complete purl stitch.

BINDING OFF

When a piece is finished, you need to get it off the needles. This is called binding off, and here is how to do it.

To bind off on the knit side:

Step One: Knit the first 2 stitches. Now insert the left needle into the first of the 2 stitches.

Draw the first stitch up and over the second stitch and completely off the needle. You have now bound off one stitch.

Step Two: Knit one more stitch; insert left needle into the first stitch on the right needle and draw it up and over the new stitch and completely off the needle. Another stitch is now bound off.

Repeat Step Two until all the stitches are bound off and one loop remains on the right-hand needle. Now to "finish off" or "end off" the yarn, cut it and draw end through the last loop to tighten.

To bind off on the purl side:

Step One: Purl the first 2 stitches. Now insert the left needle into the first stitch on the right needle, and draw it up and over the second stitch and completely off the needle. You have now bound off one stitch.

Step Two: Purl one more stitch; insert the left needle into the first stitch on the right needle and draw it over the new stitch and completely off the needle. Another stitch is bound off.

Repeat Step Two until all stitches are bound off; then finish off.

YARN OVER

To make a yarn over (an extra lp on needle) before a knit stitch:

Bring the yarn to the front of the work as if you were going to purl, then take it over the right needle to the back into the position for knitting; then knit the next stitch.

To make a yarn over before a purl stitch

Bring the yarn around the right needle from front to back over the needle, then to front again under the needle into position for purling; purl the next stitch.

INCREASING

Increasing is a shaping technique in which stitches are added, making the knitted piece wider. The most commonly used method to work an increase is to knit (or purl) twice into the same stitch.

To increase in a knit stitch

Step One: Insert the tip of right needle into the stitch from front to back as to knit; now knit the stitch in the usual manner but don't remove the stitch from the left needle.

Step Two: Insert the right needle (from front to back) into the back loop of the same stitch, and knit it again, this time slipping the stitch off the left needle.

You have now increased one stitch.

To increase in a purl stitch

Step One: Insert the right needle into the stitch from back to front as to purl;

now purl the stitch in the usual manner but don't remove the stitch from the left needle.

Step Two: Insert the right needle (from back to front) into the back loop of the same stitch and purl it again, this time slipping the stitch off the left needle.

You have now increased one stitch.

Another method for increasing stitches is called "yarn over" and is used for a decorative increase. This method should only be used when it is called for in the pattern since it leaves a small decorative hole in the work.

Yarn over between 2 knit stitches

Bring the yarn to the front of the work as if you were going to purl, then take it over the right needle to the back of the work. Yarn is now in position to knit the next stitch, and you have added one stitch.

Yarn over between 2 purl stitches

Bring the yarn over the right needle to the back of the work, then bring the yarn forward between the needles to the front of the work. The yarn is now in position to purl the next stitch, and you have added one stitch.

DECREASING

Decreasing is another shaping technique in which stitches are removed, making the knitted piece narrower. The first method of decreasing most commonly used is knitting or purling two stitches together and is worked simply by knitting (or purling) 2 stitches as one.

To knit 2 stitches together

This method, abbreviated K2 tog, is worked by inserting the right needle through the fronts of the first 2 stitches on the left needle as if to knit.

Then knit these 2 stitches as one, and you have decreased one stitch.

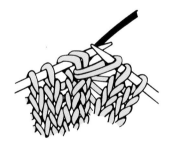

To purl 2 stitches together

This method abbreviated, P2 tog, is worked by inserting the right needle through the fronts of the next 2 stitches on the left needle as to purl. Then purl these 2 stitches as one, and you have decreased one stitch.

Passing the slipped stitch over, abbreviated PSSO, is the second most commonly used method for decreasing. It is often used in shaping where a definite decrease line is desired. The action of slipping a stitch transfers a stitch from the left needle to the right needle without working it.

To slip a stitch as to knit

Insert the right needle into the stitch on the left needle as if you were going to knit it. Instead of knitting, slip the stitch from the left needle to the right needle.

To slip a stitch as to purl

Insert the right needle into the stitch on the left needle as if you were going to purl it. Instead of purling, slip the stitch from the left needle to the right needle.

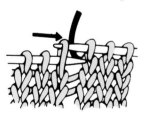

Note: Always slip a stitch as to knit unless otherwise specified in instructions

To work PSSO

Slip the next stitches as to knit; then knit the following stitches. Pass the slipped stitch over the knitted stitch by using the point of the left needle to lift the slipped stitch over the knitted stitch as in binding off.

WEAVING IN ENDS

When you finish your project, all of the yarn ends should be woven in securely. To do this, use a size 16 tapestry needle or a plastic yarn needle and weave the yarn ends through the backs of the stitches, first weaving about 2" in one direction and then I" in the reverse direction. Cut off excess yarn.

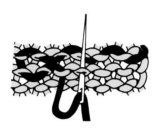

GAUGE

This is probably the most important aspect of knitting!

GAUGE simply means the number of stitches per inch, and the number of rows per inch that result from a specified yarn worked with needles in a specified size. But since everyone knits differently—some loosely, some tightly, some in-between—the measurements of individual work can vary greatly, even when the knitters use the same pattern and the same size yarn and needles.

If you don't work to the gauge specified in the pattern, your knitted projects will never be the correct size, and you may not have enough yarn to finish your project.

Needle sizes given in instructions are merely guides, and should never be used without making a 4" square sample swatch to check your gauge. It is your reponsiblity to make sure you achieve the gauge specified in the pattern.

To achieve the gauge specified, you may need to use a different needle size—either larger or smaller—than that

specified in the pattern. If you have more stitches or rows per inch than specified, you will have to try a size larger needle. If you have fewer stitches or rows per inch than specified, you will have to try a size smaller needle. Always change to larger or smaller needles if necessary to achieve gauge.

CROCHETING

Crochet is often used as a finishing technique on knitted garments.

To start, make a slip knot on the hook, leaving a 4" yarn tail.

Join by pulling the yarn through the specified knit stitch and through the loop on the hook.

To make a chain stitch (ch): YO hook from back to front, hook yarn and draw through the loop on the hook. One chain stitch made.

To work a single crochet stitch (sc):

Step 1: YO hook from back to front, and draw through the 2 loops on the hook

Step 2: Hook the yarn and draw through the 2 loops: one single crochet made.

To work a double crochet stitch (dc):

Step 1: Bring the yarn once over the hook; insert the hook in the top loop of the 4th chain from the hook.

Hook the yarn and draw through (3 loops on hook).

Step 2: Hook yarn and draw through first 2 loops on the hook.

Step 3: Hook yarn again and draw through last 2 loops on hook: one double crochet made

To work a half double crochet stitch (hdc)

Step 1: Bring the yarn over the hook. Insert the hook in the top loop of the 3rd chain from the hook. Hook yarn and draw through (3 loops now on hook).

Step 2: Hook yarn and draw through all 3 loops on the hook: one half double crochet made

FRINGE

Basic Instructions

Cut a piece of cardboard about 6" wide and half as long as specified in the instructions for strands plus ½" for trimming allowance. Wind the yarn loosely and evenly lengthwise around cardboard. When the card is filled, cut the yarn across one end. Do this several times; then begin fringing. You can wind additional strands as you need them.

Single Knot Fringe

Hold the specified number of strands for one knot of fringe together, then fold in half.

Hold the knitted project with the right side facing you. Using a crochet hook, draw the folded ends through the space or stitch from right to wrong side.

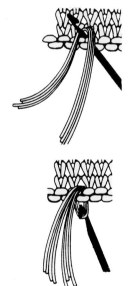

Pull the loose ends through the folded section.

Draw the knot up firmly.

Space the knots as indicated in the pattern instructions. Trim the ends of the fringe evenly.

KNITTING NEEDLES CONVERSION CHART

U.S.	0	1	2	3	4	5	6	7	8	9	10	10½	11	13	15	17
METRIC	2	2.25	2.75	3.25	3.5	3.75	4	4.5	5	5.5	6	6.5	8	9	10	12.75

ABBREVIATIONS AND SYMBOLS

Knitting patterns are written in a special shorthand, which is used so that instructions don't take up too much space. They sometimes seem confusing, but once you learn them, you'll have no trouble following them.

These are standard abbreviations

beg . . . . beginning
BO . . . . bind off
CO. cast on
ch . . . . chain
dec . . . . decrease
est . . . . established
Fig . . . . figure
inc . . . . increase(ing)
K. . . . . knit
lp(s). . . . . loop(s)
P. . . . . purl
patt . . . . pattern
prev . . . . previous
PSSO . . . . pass the slipped stitch over
PSSO2. . pass the slipped stitch over 2 sts
rem . . . . remain(ing)
rnd(s) . . . . round(s)
rep . . . . repeat(ing)
sc. . . . . single crochet
sk . . . . skip
sl . . . . slip
sp(s) . . . . space(s)
SSK. . . . . slip, slip, knit
st(s) . . . . stitch(es)
stock st . . . . stockinette stitch
tbl. . . . . through back loop
tog. . . . . together

YO. . . . . yarn over the needle
YRN. . . . . yarn around needle

These are standard symbols

* An asterisk (or double asterisks******) in a pattern row, indicates a portion of instructions to be used more than once. For instance, "rep from * three times" means that after working the instructions once, you must work them again three times for a total of 4 times in all.

† A dagger (or double daggers ††) indicates those instructions that will be repeated again later in the same row or round.

: The number after a colon tells you the number of stiches you will have when you have completed the row or round.

( ) Parentheses enclose instructions which are to be worked the number of times following the parentheses. For instance, "(K1, P2) 3 times" means that you knit one stitch and then purl two stitches, three times.

[ ] Brackets and **( )** parentheses are also used to give you additional information, for instance [rem sts are left unworked].

These are standard terms

Finish Off – This means to end your piece by pulling the yarn through the last loop remaining on the needle. This will prevent the work from unraveling.

Work Even – This means that the work is continued in the pattern as established without increasing or decreasing.

Continue in Pattern as Established – This means to follow the pattern stitch as it has been set up, working any increases or decreases in such a way that the established pattern remains the same as it was established.

Right Side – This means the side of the garment that will be seen.

Wrong Side – This means the side of the garment that is inside when the garment is worn.

Right Front – This means the part of the garment that will be worn on the right side of the body

Left Front – This means the part of the garment that will be worn on the left side of the body

The patterns in this book have been written using the knitting and crochet terminology that is used in the United States. Terms which may have different equivalents in other parts of the world are listed below

United States	International
Single crochet (sc)	double crochet (dc)
Slip stitch (sl st)	single crochet
Skip	miss
Gauge	tension
Yarn over (YO)	Yarn forward (yfwd) or Yarn around needle (yrn)

Carol Wilson Mansfield, Art Director

James Jaeger, Photography

Al Seidman, Photography

Graphic Solutions, inc-chgo, Book Design

All the garments and projects in this book were tested to ensure the accuracy and clarity of the instructions. We are grateful to the following pattern testers:

Kathy Christensen

Judy Demain

Patricia Honaker

Jodi Lewanda

Wendy Meier

Sandy Scoville

Susie Adams Steele

We also extend thanks and appreciation to these contributing designers:

Kim Britt

Jodi Lewanda

Sandy Scoville

Susie Adams Steele

Whenever we have used a specialty yarn, we have given the brand name. If you are unable to find these yarns locally, write to the following manufacturers who will be able to tell you where to purchase their products, or consult their internet sites. We also wish to thank these companies for supplying yarn for this book:

Bernat Yarns
320 Livingston Avenue South
Listowel, Ontario
Canada N4W 3H3
www.bernat.com

Crystal Palace Yarns
2320 Bissell Avenue
Richmond, California 94804
www.straw.com

Knit One, Crochet Too, Inc,
7 Commons Avenue, Suite 2
Windham, Maine 04062
www.knitonecrochettoo.com

Lion Brand Yarn Company
34 West 15th Street
New York, New York 10011
www.LionBrand.com

Patons Yarns
320 Lvingstone Avenue South
Listowel, Ontario
Canada N4Q 3H3
www.patonsyarns.com

Red Heart Yarns
Coats and Clark
Consumer Services
P.O.Box 12229
Greenville, South Carolina 29612-0229

TLC Yarns
Coats and Clark
Consumer Services
P.O.Box 12229
Greenville, South Carolina 29612-0229
www.coatsandclark.com

Every effort has been made to ensure the accuracy of these instructions.
We cannot be responsible for human error or variations in your work.

INDEX (bold face entries indicate pattern pages)

continued on page 128